*To Bret*
*Paul*

D1487176

# PERFORM

*An **NFL Coach** trains
with a **Concert Pianist**
and offers lessons on elite performance*

**www.perform-coach.com**
*also available for Kindle,
eBook apps and iBookstore.*

## PAUL ALEXANDER

**Library of Congress Number**
**2011910415**

BISAC Code: 027000
Self Help/Personal Growth/Success

**www.perform-coach.com**

The Greek Key... the ancient  symbol
representing infinity and unity.

*Dedicated to Albert in appreciation*

*To all those in the arena*

# Table of Contents

# The Inevitable

My journey with Albert, my piano teacher of two years, suddenly got serious. Michael Chertock, the Chair of the Piano Department at the University of Cincinnati's College Conservatory of Music (CCM) asked me to perform at Pianopalooza, the premier piano event of the year.

*Pianopalooza* .....*Gasp!*

The CCM piano faculty members are highly skilled concert pianists who perform professionally throughout the world. At Pianopalooza, the maestri come together to perform in this grand piano event. The house would be full of educated piano critics, perhaps a thousand of them. I accepted his invitation knowing that if I approached this difficult challenge properly, I would emerge as a better football coach ... and a better student of human performance.

My first performance was for an adult recital at CCM with 20 people in the audience. I played Beethoven's "Moonlight Sonata". It wasn't a positive experience. It was the first time I played in public, which was frightening; but, I knew the music cold. The bigger issue was that I had never played a Steinway piano before, much less a Steinway Concert Grand. Steinway is the piano's version of a violin's Stradivarius; *there is no piano like a Steinway*. As I approached the piano, my respect for the great instrument intimidated me. After all, a new one costs over $130,000.

*I wasn't afraid to look, just to touch it.*

As I began to play, the beautiful sound coming from the Steinway actually startled me. As I tried to play even more beautifully, my concentration lapsed as I focused on the sonorous piano rather than the performance of the music. As I lapsed, my nerves took over as my forearms tightened, and I slowly began to freeze. My mind wandered as my focus shifted to the audience's reaction to my music, which felt tightening as well. The moment before my hands locked up completely, my competitiveness took over as my mind kicked into a third person mentality.

*Come on, you're Paul Alexander, damn it…..not some chump!*

That third-person thought infused enough energy for me to finish the piece. I raced to the end, disregarding tempo, just to get this miserable performance over with in order to spare both the audience and myself. The experience was so traumatic that my arms, shoulders and hands were stiff and sore for days. Hard to imagine, but true!

How could 20 people in the audience and pieces of wood, metal and felt intimidate me? Stressful situations have never affected me. After all, I've coached in the NFL for 20 seasons and major college football for 10 seasons prior to that. I've coached in front of crowds exceeding 100,000 people and millions of viewers on television. I've spoken before large crowds at seminars my entire career and I've coached the Prima Donnas (actually Primo Uomini) of professional football. I have never felt intimidated. But, this piano performance skill was different. The stress of this novice pianist getting up in front of people and playing was literally daunting.

In my second performance at CCM, I fared no better. It was also at a small adult recital, and I performed Beethoven's 'Für Elise'. I decided to play it from memory, without sheet music, since I knew the music well. I also was excited about the challenge; but, I still wasn't fond of playing in front of an audience. On that particular day, I was unable to practice the piece before the recital and I attempted it cold. Not good. Once again, my hands locked up then shook; this time so violently that I had to stop. I tried to start over again, but ultimately had to completely stop. I got up from the piano, and sullenly walked back to my seat. While I was embarrassed, Albert was mad.

"You may not stop," Albert said after the recital. "You can never start over. No matter what, you must keep playing!"

*I was ashamed.*

*How can it be this hard?*

**Pianopalooza**. Albert and I were going to perform as partners on the same piano. It's called piano music for four hands. Unfortunately, Albert didn't have three of the hands.

*Was I nuts?*

My wife, Kathy, was convinced that *nuts I was*. She's known that for awhile. Albert was hopeful; but, he also knew my track record wasn't good. I was aware that the experience could likely result in complete embarrassment. Nonetheless, together we were determined to "kill" the performance. We had a month to prepare.

# CAROLYN'S LESSONS

Carolyn was in the fourth grade when she began studying piano at the University of Cincinnati's College Conservatory of Music (CCM). CCM is one of the top music conservatories in America. My wife, Kathy, and I are casual musicians; but, our daughter Carolyn is a very talented musician. It was recommended by her piano teacher that she study at the Conservatory.

I remember Carolyn's very first lesson at CCM. Her teacher, Albert Mühlböck, was a concert pianist. Austrian born and trained in Vienna, he has performed all over the world and recorded professionally. I recall doing a Google search of Albert which led me to Amazon and to a preview of a Mühlböck recording.

"Kathy, come listen to this guy ….he sounds like Horowitz". I shouted, referencing the great Russian pianist.

Later, I learned that Albert sounded more like Artur Schnabel or Alfred Brendel: concert pianists trained in the rich Austrian tradition. Nonetheless, Albert was a student at CCM completing his doctorate in piano performance. I couldn't ask for a more impressive person to teach my fourth grade daughter to play the piano. At that first lesson, I asked Albert if Carolyn's current lesson books were sufficient for her piano study with him.

"The music books are unimportant", said Albert in his rich Germanic accent. "I will teach your daughter how to play the piano."

His statement was delivered with the finality of a Mozart cadence. I knew right away that this guy was a good teacher. I admire teachers who can teach beyond the syllabus, without notes, or in my case without the crutch of a playbook. Such teachers have embraced their craft and their subject matter so well that it is part of their souls. It was that first day when my curiosity about Albert began. As I sat through her weekly lessons with him, a myriad of thoughts raced through my mind:

> *Is there any physical skill more difficult to perform than the requirements of a concert pianist?* On a typical evening, Albert might play 20,000 notes. The range of notes can span the length of the keyboard with blazing scales, glissandos and arpeggios, strong chords and gentle ornaments. The rhythms are difficult, often times the right and left hands are playing in unrelated rhythm patterns at the same time. The endurance of the music can be brutal with the pianist's arms and shoulders begging for relief. It's an athletic event which requires mental focus and physical precision that inevitably leads to perspiration and exhaustion by the end of the performance. If the pianist misses just a

few notes, he's had a bad night.

The skill of the concert pianist is able to make his piano sing like a beautiful violin. The piano is not like a typewriter or even an organ. The pressure, weight and speed applied to a key have a profound effect on the sound a key makes. The multiple techniques a pianist uses for striking and releasing the keys to create expression separates the concert pianist from the typical church organist. *How does the pianist learn and train the various techniques for performance?*

*How does he control his nerves?* Vladimir Horowitz, considered to be one of the greatest Pianists of the 20th Century, had to be coerced and pushed out of the green room and onto the stage at different points of his career. Glenn Gould, one of the greatest Bach pianists of all time, hated the pressure of performing. Gould refused to play on stage in front of an audience and limited his art to recording studios. Both Horowitz and Gould, during points of their careers, could not overcome the stress of concert performance. When the pianist gets nervous, his hands shake as he approaches disaster. It's impossible to generate great sound, if any sound at all, when the hands are shaking.

Typically, concert pianists memorize their music as a matter of practice. *How does the pianist memorize an hour or more of music that can be brutally athletic and requires enormous dexterity and focus?* One momentary mental or physical lapse and the house of cards comes tumbling down.

These thoughts became a plan. I decided to take piano lessons from Albert and train as a concert pianist. My piano experience to this point included just a dozen lessons in my lifetime, but I had enjoyed plucking at the keys since high school. I've enjoyed classical music as a hobbyist for as long as I could remember. But most importantly, I was going to find some answers to my questions about elite performance. As I began my journey with Albert, I was convinced that this football coach was going to learn a great deal about human performance.

# INGENUITY

Albert's words from Carolyn's first lesson stuck in my head:

"The music books are unimportant .I will teach your daughter how to play the piano".

As I continued to observe Carolyn's lessons with Albert, I found him to be more than profound and more than a skilled pianist.  As a singer and guitar player, I had some musical training through school. I found Albert's instructions ingenious because he was able to teach very difficult concepts in an easy way that even a fourth grader could understand. *He made difficult musical concepts appear easy.*

His lessons were so inspiring that I felt the urge to applaud at the end of each hour.  At the conclusion of Carolyn's third lesson, I mentioned to Albert:

"You're a genius".

Albert, a very humble man, nodded with an expression of both apprehension and joy.  Perhaps Albert thought I was exaggerating.  *I wasn't.*

"Genius" is a word used too casually today.

Sister    Mary    was    my    brilliant    Algebra    and

Trigonometry teacher at Cardinal Mooney High School in Rochester, New York. She was very intelligent and possessed the required traits of a model nun. Her black habit highlighted her tough, mean, focused and disciplined temperament. In Math class, she could dazzle the class with her lengthy proofs and derivations that would circle around the classroom's chalkboards. *Wow!* Unfortunately, I didn't understand any of it. Sister Mary was a brilliant mathematician who could compound the difficulty of a problem with a lengthy, confusing solution. Sister Mary had little regard for simplicity. She was a brilliant woman. Not a genius.

In my view, *a genius finds simple solutions to complex problems.*

I love pizza. There is nothing more frustrating than a delivered pie with the box crushed into the cheese from the weight of several pizze stacked on top of it. The guy who invented the plastic tripod that has prevented this genocide of millions of pizze was a genius.

Albert Einstein purportedly developed his theory of relativity by watching a window washer travel outside of his office window. He explained his complex theory by stating that speed was relative to the situation. If one is standing still and observes a train speeding past him, then he assumes that the train is going fast. If that same observer was traveling alongside that same speeding train, he would assume that the train is standing still. Einstein, through his use of simple **thought experiments,** was able to postulate solutions to large, and even cosmic issues. Einstein was a genius.

Paul Brown, the legendary Hall of Fame Coach, was the successful coach and founder of both the Cleveland Browns (his namesake) and the Cincinnati Bengals. Paul Brown was certainly one of the most innovative, ingenious coaches in the history of the game. He invented playbooks, full time assistant coaches, scouts, the facemask, the draw play, the 40 yard dash, and IQ testing for draft prospects. Brown's contributions included systems, procedures, inventions, strategies and social ideas that would shape the future thought of the National Football League.

I found Paul Brown's sage advice to assistant coach Bruce Coslet to be ingenious:

"If you want to be heard, speak softly."

I remember vividly in my youth when bottled water first hit the market. It seemed ridiculous that someone would buy bottled water when it was readily available at drinking fountains for free. But the guy who went to his boss with the belief that they could sell bottled water, while his co-workers in the background were likely snickering, was a genius. So was his boss who listened.

Are you the type of person who knows why the number "57" is etched on the neck of a bottle of Heinz ketchup ™? I've asked this question at seminars for years and typically about five percent of the people in the audiences know the answer. Perhaps the "57" represents the number of ingredients in the recipe, but why the location? It's placed at the precise spot where if one taps gently on the tipped bottle, the ketchup flows freely from the bottle. Even the new plastic squeeze bottles have a perfectly placed "57" at its optimal squeezing position. The person who figured that out was a genius.

When I see a large football player turn a bottle of ketchup upside down and pound at its heel with tremendous force yet with limited success, I immediately make the mental note:

*He must either play defensive line, or if he plays offensive line, he can't play for me.*

I'm an Offensive Line Coach. I coach the big, fat guys, and I love them. Offensive linemen need to be the smartest, most cohesive group on the football field because they are responsible for the combinations of problems that eleven coordinated defenders can cause. In football, there are eleven defenders and eight gaps that they can charge. Assuming each man can choose one gap, there are 437,514 possible defensive alignments that the offensive line must deal with. Football strategy can be complicated much like an advanced level math problem. Offensive linemen and their coaches seek to solve complex problems with simple solutions.

Inventors, by definition, are ingenious. Shunpei Yamazaki, the Japanese inventor, holds 1432 United States Patents in his name, the most patents of any individual. Most of his work involves inventions in the electronics industry.

Yamazaki probably once said: 私は発明家である

Perhaps we can relate easier to the American inventor, Thomas Edison, the holder of 1093 United States Patents. Edison produced breakthrough inventions such as the light bulb, the movie camera and the phonograph. Interestingly, most people believe that Edison holds the most U.S. Patents. Edison, however, doesn't even hold the record for the most U.S. Patents by an American. Donald Weever holds 1321 patents. Most of Weever's patents are related to packaging floral arrangements.

Neither Yamazaki nor Weever is a renowned wordsmith of the English language. While Edison no longer holds the record for the most U.S. Patents, he certainly offers the most inspiring quote.

"I have not failed," said Edison. "I've just found 10,000 ways that won't work."

Edison's quote hangs above my desk and is a daily inspiration to me.

J.S. Bach is regarded today as the quintessential Baroque era composer (1685-1750). After Bach, the next most salient composer to enter the stage was W.A. Mozart (1756 - 1791) who helped define the Classical Era in music. Mozart wrote music that perhaps could be more pleasant to listen to.... longer, cleaner melodies with a predictable formality. Both the Baroque Period and the Classical Period had clearly defined, distinct rules of the order, style, tonality and rhythm attributed to their music. After Mozart came Beethoven.

Ludwig van Beethoven's genius was to fuse the two philosophies of music that were believed to be incompatible opposites into a new form. Furthermore, Beethoven expanded those limits of order, style, tonality and rhythm in a way that inspired the next period of music – the Romantic Era. Many musicologists believe that Beethoven cannot be defined by a musical era. He wasn't Baroque; he wasn't Classical nor was he Romantic. He was all periods of tonal music in one. Beethoven is best described as the bridge between the Classical and Romantic Eras. My favorite composer is Beethoven. When I listen to Beethoven, I can hear Bach, Mozart and Brahms (sometimes even Gershwin) all at the same time.

> Countess Anna Maria Erdody was a brilliant student of Beethoven's and a close friend. The Countess, who was experiencing depression due to the loss of a child, came to Beethoven for consolation. Beethoven sat at the piano and began speaking with his fingers. His music spoke. If I could have a conversation with any person in history, I would choose Beethoven …. provided that he brought his piano. I have a few questions for him.

Ludwig's personality, on the other hand, was outrageous, tumultuous and perhaps psychotic. His music was said to parallel his personality. Beethoven believed that the greater the tension in music, the sweeter the resolution. Beethoven would push the listener to his limit with sharp, intense tone contrasts and then resolve into heavenly music in a euphoric way. His music was metaphysical and one could argue that he was a philosopher as much as he was a musician. Or was he psychotic? [My response …. *Opus 111. Amen.*]

Beethoven was a genius in every way. He had a clear vision; his brilliance needed no interpretation; his music was completely original; and, he possessed tremendous amounts of energy as he altered the course of history.

The most ingenious offensive lineman I have ever coached .... was Willie Anderson, the Bengals' Pro Bowl right offensive tackle. Most years, Willie would surrender only one quarterback "sack" per season. Such a feat is nearly impossible. Willie, however, accomplished this feat several times. In fact, one season he even went sack-less. Willie was a four-time Pro Bowler, certainly one of the best offensive tackles in the modern era, and one of the best right offensive tackles in the history of the game. It was an honor for me to be Willie's coach for practically his entire NFL career.

Willie and I first met in Indianapolis at the NFL Combine, a tryout camp for draft-eligible players. When I interviewed him, he was a nervous 20-year-old guy excited about the future. Willie was a huge, affable man with a big heart and a whispering southern accent that I could barely understand. As one of the first offensive linemen to declare for the draft after only three years of college, he was a very young man entering an arena of full-grown gladiators.

As the interviewer, I was a baby-faced 32-year-old man, the youngest and least experienced offensive line coach in the NFL. Most NFL line coaches typically don't even get warmed up until they're 50 years old. Many coach well into their 60's and 70's, since a tremendous amount of knowledge and experience is required. I was going to be responsible for developing this great athlete into an elite NFL performer. We were perfect for each other.

Willie's career was a study in itself.   I watched; I listened; we talked; and, we experimented as we created techniques that were suited specifically for him.  It was wonderful.  He was a great talent, a man's man and a clutch performer.  Overall, we were both excited to come up with simple solutions to the complex problems that were presented on the football field. Willie was a genius.

Talking with many musicians at the Conservatory, I wasn't alone on my assessment of Albert.
Eugene Pridinoff is one of the world's top experts on piano performance and Albert's advisor for his doctoral studies.  Dr. Pridinoff once shared:

"The lessons I have with Albert are easy. He plays the music and I tell him that it's beautiful".

Because of the Conservatory, Cincinnati is fortunate to have several internationally renowned concert pianists.   Michael Chertock,  Awadagin Pratt and   Eugene and Elizabeth Pridonoff are a few  whom I have come to know.  I was ready to begin lessons with Albert….the genius, the world-class performer who would train me like a concert pianist.  My goal was not to emerge as a concert pianist; I lacked the innate talent and the amount of time necessary for such development.  But, through the process of training to be a concert pianist, I would gain insight into the common traits of great performers.

Both Willie and Albert, in my opinion, are geniuses. My journey set me in the middle of this triangle. I was the coach of an elite performer and the student of one at the same time.

While traveling this journey, I discovered that there were common traits associated with elite athletic and musical performance. I've noticed that certain thoughts are common in all physical performance. This book is a collection of those thoughts. They are presented in a shotgun manner intended to offer insight into an array of performance issues. My pleasure in composing this opus is:

- To share a musical example that enlightens an athlete.

- To offer an athletic axiom that inspires a musician.

- And to share a perspective that moves a teacher or coach to become a better performer, himself (or herself).

Hopefully, some of these thoughts can help you as you aspire to learn, teach and PERFORM!

"Simplicity is the ultimate sophistication."
**Leonardo da Vinci**

# SKILL

*Few Things are impossible to diligence and skill.*

*Samuel Johnson*

# My First Lesson

"Play something for me," Albert suggested.

Since high school, I have worked on Beethoven's "Moonlight Sonata". The sonata is the middle, slow movement of his 14th Piano Sonata Opus 27 no. 2 written in 1801. Beethoven did not name the piece "Moonlight" nor did he envision a moon as he composed it. To help promote its sales, a publicist posthumously coined the name "Moonlight" with this work. Nonetheless, the common name describes the mood as a peaceful, slowly moving fantasy that evokes passions of love and longing.

It was the piece of music I knew best. I practiced it diligently in the weeks prior to my first lesson with Albert. I was ready to wow him with my virtuosic performance. My expression would be moving. I was sure that he would tell me that it was great and we could study some new music.

I began to play. Although I was nervous, I managed to give a decent performance that I thought Albert would find inspiring.

"That's a good starting point," Albert offered. "We need to work on a number of things".

*I swallowed my pride.*

The melody line of "Moonlight" is played mostly by the pinky and ring finger of the right hand. The remaining eight fingers play arpeggios (broken chords) and baseline to provide the accompaniment (background music). The melody is like a voice singing in front of the backup singers and the band.

"I couldn't hear the melody over the accompaniment," said Albert. "It all sounded equal. You need to play the melody louder and the accompaniment softer."

I was confused. I had always just played the notes disregarding balance between the two hands. Albert was asking me to play some fingers on my right hand louder, than the other fingers on my hands, while all ten were playing simultaneously.

"In fact, each part should have a different feel in your finger tips. In this piece, I would imagine that the melody fingers feel like scissors cutting through cardboard while the accompaniment fingers feel like they are pushing on shaving cream." Albert concluded.

I replied, "So I need to play two different volumes and textures with different parts of my hands at the same time?" *This seemed insurmountable to me.*

"Actually, not really," said Albert.    "The accompaniment has two parts to it: a baseline and the middle arpeggios.  You'll need to play it as if three unique voices are singing together.    One person sings the melody while two backup singers sing the base line and the middle harmony."

My reaction to Albert was, "That seems impossible."

"It should," Albert said. "You don't know how to press the keys properly. You do everything with your fingers. I will teach you how to use your whole upper body to push weight through the keys. By pivoting your hands, you can adjust the pressure points and generate various contrasting sounds."

Maybe I'm a slow learner, but this was hard. Learning to coordinate the weakest fingers of my hand to play louder than the strongest fingers was not natural. I felt clumsy and nonathletic. I wasn't sure if I could ever accomplish such a feat.

*Albert made it look and sound so easy.*

> "Nearly every person who develops an idea works at it up to the point where it looks impossible, and then gets discouraged. That's not the place to be discouraged."
> **Thomas Edison**

# A Parable

*[**Parable** …. not a story but a message]*

One day, a landowner met with a laborer on his property.

"I would like to build my home on this spot," said the landowner. "Today I would like you to dig the foundation."

The next day, the landowner returned to the property only to find that the foundation had been dug 100 yards to the south of his planned location.

"This is wrong," said the landowner to the laborer. "Why didn't you dig it at the spot I instructed you?"

The laborer replied, "The spot that you chose was very rocky." "I found it much easier to do the job in this new area."

"No, that's not what I want," said the landowner. "Fill the hole back in and dig the foundation in the spot where I instructed."

The second day, the landowner returned to the property only to find that the foundation had been dug 100 yards to the north of his planned location, next to a beautiful shade tree.

"This is also wrong," said the landowner to the laborer. "Why didn't you dig it at the spot I instructed you?"

The laborer replied, "It was very hot yesterday." "I found it much easier to do the job in this new area, under the shade of the tree."

"No, that's not what I wanted either," said the landowner. "Fill the hole back in and dig the foundation in the spot where I instructed."

On the third day, the landowner returned to the property only to find that the hole had been dug 100 yards to the east of his planned location, overlooking a peaceful ravine.

"This is clearly wrong," said the landowner to the laborer. "Why didn't you dig it at the spot I instructed you?"

The laborer replied, "I found this peaceful ravine." "I thought you would be pleased that I chose this new area with a great view for your great home."

"No, that's not what I want," said the landowner.

"Fill the hole back in and never come back again. I will find someone else who is *coachable*."

Some hear while others listen. All coaches desire players who are great listeners and athletes who are able to accurately respond to coaching.

# The Half – Full Glass

"Is the glass half empty or is it half full?"

*Well, neither.*

I believe the glass can be exactly half. Why can't it be half? Mathematically, is zero a more negative or positive integer? It's neither. Zero is zero.

I'm a realist and I believe that feedback to performers needs to be real and accurate. I find that the more truthful I am with NFL players, the better they respond. While coaching on the field, I'm a man of few words. I try to paint a vivid picture that is accurate. Sometimes, I take long pauses before responding; the art of coaching is the skill to offer the perfectly crafted feedback, which elicits the desired response. Professional athletes demand that their coaches are honest and accurate.

The security of the relationship between the player and the coach should be real. At the beginning of each season, I share a dose of reality with my players:

"My job is to replace each of you with someone better."

My matter-of-fact, steadfast comment is usually matched with horror from the faces of the younger players. The older players, usually, nod in agreement. *They have been touched by reality.*

Rosters in professional sports are constantly changing with the intent of improving. There are several avenues for finding new players, including: free agency, the draft and unsigned "street" players looking for work. The sooner a performer understands that the coach loves him, but will replace him the moment he finds someone more talented, the better off he is. There is always someone younger and brighter with more talent and determination waiting backstage.

I also share my reality dosage with some realistic encouragement as well:

"If you become a better player yourself, then I've replaced you. We are a better team."

My optimistic comment is then usually matched with looks of informed determination.

The key to a performer's survival is his ability to continually hone his skills so that he can remain the chosen one.

> "Early laurels weigh like lead."
> **Cyril Connolly**

# Practice and Priorities

How does an NFL football coach work 70+ hour weeks and learn the piano at the same time?  It's easy.... don't sleep. During the season, I come home at night and everyone in my family is asleep. When I leave in the morning, they are still sleeping. For obvious reasons, I've made the statement:

"All you people do around here is sleep!"

The truth is that when I come home from work, the last thing I can do is sleep.  I need to unwind in a way that takes my mind off of football.  I believe it's critical to clear my mind so I can create new thoughts and ideas.  So, I practice the piano at midnight.  Obviously, there are some problems with pounding on a six-foot grand piano when everyone is sleeping.

Consequently, I choose to play only lullaby-type music so that my family's dreams are pleasant. You might find it odd that a rugged football coach plays only sweet music, but I adjust to my situation.  I would love to play Rachmaninoff's powerful Prelude in C# minor, but everyone would have nightmares.

*Specializing in a single style of music can restrict a performer's opportunities.  At this point, my music selections are more suited for weddings than divorces.*

When my oldest daughter, Mary Beth, went away to college, she had one request for a special gift.

*Uh, oh, here it goes...* I thought as the visions of dollar signs danced in my head.

"Dad," asked Mary Beth, "I'm afraid I won't be able to sleep without hearing you play the piano at night. Would you make a CD of your music for me?"

Those daughters know how to drive a stake through their father's heart.

> "And the night shall be filled with music,
> And the cares that infest the day
> Shall fold their tents like Arabs
> And as silently steal away."
> **Henry Wadsworth Longfellow**

# Trust your Eyes

In 1992, during my rookie NFL coaching season, I saw the trading card of Pro Bowl Tackle Gary Zimmerman of the Denver Broncos. The photo on his card showed Gary in the act of pass blocking. His hands were set down low, not held high in front of his chest which is the way the proper technique would read in a coaching textbook. I was young and a self-anointed "expert" fresh from coaching college football. *I was shocked*.

"Zimmerman is one of the best offensive linemen in football," I thought, "and he doesn't even know how to position his hands properly for pass protection."

As I continued to watch great players, I saw that they all held their hands in exactly the same position. A few years ago, I spent an evening searching for Google images of NFL offensive linemen pass blocking. [*Certainly I could find someone who held his hands the way the textbooks teach.*] After scrutinizing hundreds of photos, every single player set with his hands in this *unsound* position. I made the decision to stop coaching a textbook technique that obviously was not used during elite performance. Zimmerman was right.

By their nature, coaches can be skeptical. I've told this story about hand placement at coaching clinics for several years. During my talks, I can feel the coaches' expressions of doubt. The coaches, however, become converted when they see my photos of great offensive linemen like: Jonathan Ogden, Willie Anderson, Tony Boselli, Orlando Pace, Willie Roaf, Chris Samuels and Anthony Munoz holding their hands similarly. Even skeptical football coaches like evidence. They, too, trust their eyes.

A lot can be learned from simply watching. Once a new technique is observed, it becomes discovered; when the discovery is assigned a name, it becomes an invention. My favorite invented term is **declusterfication**. Declusterfication is the conversion of a man-blocking scheme into a zone-blocking concept. Typically, pairs of blockers are assigned to clusters of defenders. In certain circumstances, the blockers de-cluster and block areas rather than their assigned men. De-clusterfication is an example of a catchy, made-up term that both the coach and the player can embrace to identify a specific situation.

A critical observation of a casual event is one of life's spices. I agree with the creative philosopher and semanticist Yogi Berra:

*"You can observe a lot just by watching."*

Most people are aware of the invention of Post-it Notes™. A researcher at 3M, Spencer Silver, inadvertently developed glue that did not bind effectively. The glue, however, was able stick to paper; the paper could then be "posted". Silver tried unsuccessfully to promote his invention for years. His idea was later fulfilled when Arthur Fry, another 3M scientist, used Silver's product to mark pages in his church hymnal. The *faux pas* discovery became a brilliant invention.

Over a half century ago, the Cleveland Browns invented the **draw** play. The draw is a deception play that initially appears to be a pass play by the actions of the blockers and the backfield. After the defense reacts to the pass action, the quarterback hands the ball to the running back as he runs straight ahead with the ball. Few people are aware of the origin of the draw play.

The draw play, like Post-it Notes™, was discovered purely by accident. In the 1940's, the Cleveland Browns were playing the Miami Seahawks in an All American Conference game. Cleveland's Quarterback Otto Graham called for a trap play in the huddle. After the ball was snapped, the play was fouled up and the timing was delayed. As Graham inadvertently bumped into running back Marion Motley, he became startled; Graham handed Motley the ball. Motley converted the busted play for good yardage. Rather than dismissing this anomaly as an accidental stroke of good fortune, Coach Paul Brown and his staff adjusted the blocking assignments and developed the modern draw play.

Invention by accident is the brilliant act of discovery.

"Doubt is the father of invention."
**Galileo**

# Photocognition

"Pieta", sculpted by a youthful Michelangelo, can be found in St. Peter's Basilica in the Vatican. The sculpture depicts Mary holding the dead body of Jesus. I had seen photos of this marvelous piece of art; the photos, however, offer an incomplete message. When I experienced "Pieta" in person, I was stunned by the lack of balance between the body sizes of Mary and the Christ. Mary is much larger than Jesus. The subject for "Pieta" is not about the death of Jesus; the scope is about the "pity" and agony of the mother towards her broken son. Perspective.

Perspective can be blurred. To look at Michelangelo's statue "David", it is striking to note the disproportional relationship between his body and his extremities. The giant killer's head, hands and feet are huge. "David" was sculpted with the intent of being placed high on the façade of the Basilica di Santa Maria del Fiore. David's extremities, from a distance, would appear balanced with the rest of his body. But, when viewed from close proximity, Michelangelo's subject appears to lack balance. Artists are masters at the manipulation of perspective.

Perspective to the artist includes: size, shape, textures and colors. Perspective to the musician includes: tones, dynamics, tempi and articulations. Perspective to the coach is his ability to visually evaluate players, techniques and games so that he can make decisions and adjustments. Perspective defines art.

*Photocognition* is a useful coaching technique that I developed years ago. It's a common sense skill for those who coach, teach and evaluate performance. Many times a player's technique will fail him and the coach is confounded. Typically, if the coach fails to note a   fault on the first observance, then he is unable to know the cause for the error. Photocognition is a skill that allows the coach to review the event repeatedly until an error is identified.   The skill is pretty straightforward; but, it requires some mental discipline from the coach to execute it effectively.

The technique of photocognition came to me shortly after my first game as a rookie NFL coach. In 1992, during the preseason opener,  I was seated in the press box as our New York Jets were playing the Philadelphia Eagles.  My coaching assignment was to identify which defender tackled our running back on each play and to communicate that information to Head Coach Bruce Coslet over the headphones.  The first play of the game was an off tackle play to the left for a short gain.

"Paul, who made the tackle?" asked Coach Coslet.

*Pause*

"I have no idea."

The speed of the NFL game is so fast that a novice is overwhelmed. I remember adapting a skill that I used as a baseball umpire years earlier. Once the pitch or the play began, I withheld all judgments and distractions until the skill was performed in its entirety. In effect, I record the event with my eyes being the camera lens and my brain being the hard drive memory. Once recorded, I can slowly replay the performance back and forth in my mind until I discover the fault.

I've talked about photocognition at seminars for many years. Recently, I've offered a twist which I call *advanced photocognition*. I preface the concept with the assumption that great teachers and coaches are like painters whose art is painted in their minds before their canvas. When observing a skill, the elite teacher is able to sketch in his mind what the skill should look like before it is performed. By visualizing the correct movement before it happens, the coach is able to "overlay" the sketched standard on top of the actual recorded event. As the coach observes and replays the recorded event, he is able to offer accurate and specific feedback.

Finally, as a coach, I'm able to perform every football technique that I teach. I can feel blocking in my bones and when a defender creates a problem, I can feel the problem. I encourage all coaches to be able to feel the skills they teach in their own bodies and learn how to perform them correctly. Nothing looks worse than a coach's demonstration of a skill that is filled with technical faults. The coach's credibility is compromised.

> "A beautiful thing never gives so much pain as does failing to hear and see it."
> **Michelangelo**

# Audiocognition

Photocognition is a **hapax legomenon**, i.e. a word that is an original idea that can only be found in one language and possesses a single meaning. Contemporary hapax legomena examples would be: LOL, BTW and TTYL. Who would have thought that texting language could be so exciting to etymologists? [*ok! … back to performance*]

"I like the term photocognition," Robert Greenberg told me.

Robert Greenberg Ph.D. is a composer, musicologist and teacher. Bob is a Princeton graduate and a former faculty member at the University of California at Berkeley and the San Francisco Conservatory. I have been a student in his classroom for at least a dozen different college level courses in Musicology. His classroom can be found in my car as well as in the cars of thousands of other students. Bob teaches via audio and video (CDs/DVDs) that are produced by *The Teaching Company.* Some course topics include: <u>The Symphonies of Beethoven</u> (32 lectures), <u>The Concerto</u> (24 lectures) and <u>How to Listen to and Understand Great Music</u> (32 lectures). Bob's scholarship and instruction is brilliant, entertaining, provoking, funny and ingenious. For most of a year, I sat in Bob's classroom for 90 minutes each day during my commute to and from work.

While in the process of writing this book, I contacted Bob and asked if he would review my draft. His insights and expertise were fantastic. It's from Bob's lectures that I've learned about: hapax legomenon, primo uomini and maestri. [Italians don't order pizzas; the plural of pizza is pizze.] I've also learned that vocalists sing songs; instruments are incapable of singing and instrumental music is referred to as a piece or a number. I've also learned music history, theory, sociology and composition from hundreds of his lectures.

"I have a new word for you....*audiocognition*," Dr. Greenburg offered.

"When I conduct, I hear the music in my head several measures (seconds) before the orchestra plays it. I compare the anticipated sound in my head with the sound in my ears that is produced by the orchestra. I'm able to compare, and then offer feedback."

Albert is an expert **audiocognitionist** *[ha]*. The typical music teacher sits adjacent to his pupil during an entire individual lesson so that he can mark the errors on the score. Albert, the atypical music teacher, begins the lesson by sitting at the opposite end of the classroom while the student performs his piece. He listens, without interruption, until the piece is finished; it's a performance experience for the student. But, here's the magic: after verbally applauding, Albert points to the sections of error and addresses them with the student.  He never misses a note.

"How do you do that?" I asked Albert one day.
"How do you remember every missed note?"

"I listen to the music and keep it fresh in my ears.
As I review the score with my eyes, I remember
how you played it." Albert replied.

"That's a variation of Greenburg's practice of
audiocognition," I told Albert. *He looked confused.*

Audiocognition. *I like it.*

> "A painter paints pictures on canvas.  But
> musicians paint their pictures on silence."
> **Leopold Stowoski**

# Horowitz

Vladimir Horowitz was one of the top pianists of the 20th Century. In 1925, the 22 year old defected from Russia with the excuse of studying with Artur Schnabel. Horowitz did not return to his homeland for 61 years. In 1986, he performed monumental recitals in Moscow and St. Petersburg.

Horowitz was a magician at the keyboard by creating his own, unique sound. Observant audiophiles can recognize a Horowitz recording immediately. Horowitz traveled with his own piano and his own piano tuner, Franz Mohr. His piano was never in tune. Mohr purposely tuned the high-pitched keys on the piano sharply; it was a trick that contributed to Horowitz' famous and mysterious sound.

About 30 years ago, I remember watching Mike Wallace interview Horowitz and his wife for an episode of 60 Minutes. At that time, Horowitz rarely performed outside of his Manhattan apartment; in fact, Horowitz recorded from his living room. As I roughly recall, Wallace posed the sugary question to Mrs. Horowitz:

"Isn't it wonderful to hear the Maestro play all day long?" encouraged Wallace.

"It's terrible," replied Mrs. Horowitz. "He plays the same measures over and over again."

Wallace did not know the rest of the story. Mrs. Horowitz' maiden name was Toscanini. Her father was Arturo Toscanini, the famous conductor of the NBC Symphony Orchestra. Mrs. Toscanini-Horowitz was an elite pianist herself and Wallace, the elegant reporter, was ultimately embarrassed by his condescending question.

What does it tell you when the top pianist in the world keeps practicing the same measures over and over again? NFL players practice their basic fundamentals every day. Technique requires constant refinement and repetition. Fundamental techniques are like shaving. If you don't do it every day, eventually, you will look ragged.

Arturo Toscanini, by the way, once chastised his orchestra for playing sluggishly.

"The music says play it *con amore.* You're playing like a bunch of married old men."

*Nice.*


One of my favorite Horowitz quotes is:

"If I don't practice for a day, I know it. If I don't practice for two days, my wife knows it. If I don't practice for three days, the world knows it."

It's a popular quote and if you're a musician you've probably heard it before. But did you know that Horowitz' wife was such a qualified critic? Did you realize that even the greatest performers live in worlds of tedious rehearsals?

> "All compromise is based on give and take, but there can be no give and take on fundamentals. Any compromise on mere fundamentals is a surrender for it is all give and no take."
> **Mohandas Gandhi**

# Flat Fingers and Trenches

Beethoven had a miserable, lonely childhood. His father forced him to practice at the keyboard constantly. He was determined to make Beethoven the next Mozart, the next great child prodigy. Occasionally, young Beethoven would sneak away from the piano; his drunken father would beat him and send him back for more practice. Witnesses recalled visions of young Beethoven seated at the piano with sad, tearful eyes. This story is not an exaggeration. Beethoven practiced so hard, and so often during his formative years that it's believed that he literally disfigured the tips of his fingers. It's rumored that they were completely flat. Some postulate that this became a mechanical advantage for his performances later in life. Beethoven was a small man, yet so powerful that he would break strings, hammers and anything else that got in his way as he attacked the keyboard. Some believe that the abusive relationship between Beethoven, his father and his music led to the psychological drive to completely re-create music as it was known at that time.

> Beethoven's, "Moonlight Sonata," was not one of his favorite works. "Surely I've written better." The **Beatles** liked it though. John Lennon wrote "Because" after hearing Yoko Ono play the sonata on the piano. He just inverted the chords.

Dan Dierdorf was an All-Pro Offensive Tackle for the St. Louis Cardinals in the 1970's. The Hall of Famer's coach was Jim Hanifan, one of the great offensive line coaches in the history of the NFL. During Dan's rookie season, Coach Hanifan drilled him repetitively to develop a consistent pass set technique. These drills were boring and required hard work. Dan, currently a CBS Sports commentator, was never shy to speak; he asked the Coach when they planned to stop this repetitive training.

Coach Hanifan replied, "When your set is so consistent that your cleats have dug trenches in the ground."

Everyone knows that hard work is important. The odds of a person being struck by lightning are better than being enshrined in the Pro Football Hall of Fame or being a concert soloist at Carnegie Hall. Usually players believe that they are working hard, but inevitably they must learn to push themselves even harder as they ascend to the next level.

Joe Paterno, the legendary Penn State coach, used to tell his team:

"Success is never final. Failure is never fatal."

How true. Joe knew that it was human nature for individuals to relax when they enjoyed success; he also knew that they would tend to press when responding to failure. As a young coach working for Coach Paterno, I was surprised to observe that he was actually harder on his team after a blowout victory than a tuff loss.

> "There is nothing noble about being superior to some other man. The true nobility is in being superior to your previous self."
> **Hindu proverb**

# Grace and Tuffness

Beethoven's "Für Elise" is one of the most popular piano pieces in the repertoire of historical music. There is no definitive background information for "Fur Elise" other than it was oddly found in a locked drawer after Beethoven's death. "Für Elise" was not published in Beethoven's lifetime despite the fact that he liked money and that most of his works were published. The mystery behind "Für Elise" has led to much speculation. One popular tale is that Beethoven composed this beautiful piece as a marriage proposal to Therese Melfatti. If this account is true, then it was a brilliant move. Beethoven was much more skillful at speaking to people through his music than verbally because of his deafness and his miserable, explosive demeanor. Regardless, Therese Melfatti along with several other beautiful, aristocratic women rejected his romance.

The English translation of "Für Elise" is *For Elise*; it's believed that there was a misprint to Beethoven's title with its posthumous publication. *Elise* should have read *Therese*. Unfortunately, the score has been lost; we might never know the true story.

Most people can recognize "Für Elise" from the Charles M. Schulz television special, "A Charlie Brown Christmas". The character, Schroeder, is a music lover (particularly Beethoven) and Lucy Van Pelt is a Schroeder lover. Schulz knew his

Beethoven well.    Shultz's choice of Schroeder playing "Für Elise" as Lucy is flirting with him was brilliant irony.

I wanted to learn how to play "Für Elise".

"Albert, listen to this recording," I said.

I played a recording for him from a greatest hits type CD that I had acquired from a clearance table. It was recorded by a British pianist with a fast, machine gun-like interpretation; it was as expressively interesting as listening to paint dry. As I watched Albert's reaction, I could see that this music was sour to his ears and he wanted to spit it out.

*I trusted Albert's expertise.*    Musicians are products of their teachers as their skills are passed down from teacher to student.    A musician is often defined by his lineage of teachers.    Through Albert's training in the Viennese style, he was connected with the great German composers. After all, Albert was [roughly] Beethoven's sixth great grand student with the lineage being: Beethoven, Czerny, Liszt, von Bülow, Barth, Rossler, Hoffman and Mühlböck. I guess that made me Beethoven's seventh grand student; I'm certainly the black sheep. Once again, *I trusted Albert.*

To Albert's disappointment, "Für Elise" is often performed in a mechanical, unemotional style. It is one of the most popular ring tones for mobile phones, which I'm sure would have irked

Beethoven. [*Especially if he didn't receive a rights' fee.*] "Für Elise" begins with short, melodic pieces (motifs) which build into a long, lyrical theme. Later in the piece, dark and intense chords agitate the listener in a disturbing and unpleasant way. Ultimately, the tense section resolves by returning to the lyrical melody and the resolution is a welcomed, euphoric experience. The listener is rescued at the last second. A common thread in Beethoven's music supported his philosophy that the greater the tension in his music (and in life), the sweeter its resolution.

Albert insisted that different parts be played as intended: legato (smoothly) with tenderness, explosively with tension and brightly with harmonious resolution. Such an interpretation was Beethoven at his finest. I was determined to play "Für Elise" with an interpretation that would make Beethoven proud.

*I would play "Für Elise" as a marriage proposal.*

"Für Elise" is often a "show off" piece for child prodigies. The full keyboard is utilized and the pianist's hands jump up and down the keyboard... an impressive looking skill that tends to wow the audiences. The watered down versions are often performed at youth recitals. Most everyone knows some kid who has performed "Für Elise". However, the authentic version and interpretation of the piece is reserved for skillful pianists.

One of the devilish parts of the piece is a section where the hands jump across octave E skips as they fly up the keyboard.

"Play..." Albert encouraged as he stood at the opposite end of the classroom.

As I began the piece, I was really looking forward to the part of the octave E skips. It's very flashy and looks impressive; it's a showman's dream section. I'm sure that it was Liberace's favorite part, too. As I played the octave E skips, they were fast and fancy. My hands flew high into the air as I smashed down loudly on a decisive, final high E note. I played it in a way that would woo everyone in the audience; it would even jolt those who had fallen asleep.

*As I approached the finish, I felt proud. I felt accomplished.*

"That's a good start," Albert once again offered. "Let's talk about the octave E skips, they're all wrong."

*Once again, I swallowed my pride.*

"The Octave E's needed to be played more gently. The hands need to move quickly; but, the touch needs to be very soft. The quietest note in the entire piece needs to be the highest E. The note that you played forte (loudly)," Albert said.

"But I've heard recordings," I countered. "I've heard others play that note loudly."

"That's because it's easier to play it loudly with speed, than softly with speed and touch," Albert insisted. "The great pianists play it that way. The show-offs play it loudly and it looks impressive. Their sound is hollow."

*Graceful*

Graceful was the thought that came to my mind. Albert cares only about great sound. When he plays this piece, he makes it look very easy. He is in control and he generates glorious sound. His ability to play difficult music gracefully is the reason that he can play the virtuoso music that very few pianists can perform.

The elite performer makes his skill look easy.

*Effortless*

In our family, we have a unique birthday party tradition. Whenever our children have a birthday party with several guests, we have a gift exchange; all the kids share and take home the presents. A birthday is a gift that should be shared with others; but mostly, I don't want 30 presents cluttering up the house. For my 48th birthday, I had a party and invited 10 close friends to our home. My gift to them was to hear Albert Mühlböck perform.

My friend Bill, asked, "Can Albert play like Liberace with his hands crossing all over the place?"

"Bill, if you ask him that, then you're not invited." I deadpanned.

*Albert is my kind of performer.* He makes the very difficult things look easy. No wasted motion, no signs of stress. Certainly not like Liberace. [Wladziu Valentino Liberace was a classically trained pianist who switched styles and became a flashy entertainer. The flamboyant showman during the 1950's to 1970's was the highest paid entertainer in the world.] My joy came on my birthday from watching jaws drop, as my guests were five feet away from a concert pianist for the first time in their lives. Watching Albert was as inspiring as watching a Gold Medal Olympic performance.

Prior to coaching in the NFL, I perceived pro football to lack intensity. Pro ball. I never really saw bodies flying around on the ground with relentless effort.

*The NFL appeared to lack the college spirit.*

I thought that the pros didn't play as hard, maybe because they were getting paid so much money. I hear these same thoughts from others today.

NFL football, on the contrary, is a tuff sport. The sounds of pads hitting, the grunting and groaning that you hear on highlight programs are not piped in noises. They are real and intense; NFL football has an intense sound to it. Towards the end of training camp, I can tell when the team is ready to play regular season games by the players' crisp, percussive sounds that they've developed during practice.

Willie Anderson was a great player and, perhaps, the most defining thought of Willie is:

*Willie made blocking look easy.*

You might say Willie was a minimalist. Willie refined his technique so well that he eliminated all unnecessary movements. He played the game with his body in a compact, balanced posture. His feet and hand strikes were controlled and deliberate. He wasn't a fish out of water.

I now realize that the reason NFL football might look more controlled than college football is because the athletes are better and more graceful. They can stay on their feet and maintain their balance longer. Balance and grace allows NFL athletes to generate more powerful blocks and tackles. I often share with my players the thought that:

*More power comes from relaxed muscles than clenched teeth.*

Grace, intensity and tuffness are traits of NFL football. Tuffness is the hardest of the traits to evaluate in NFL prospects; but, it is absolutely necessary for survival in the NFL's gladiator arena. Above the door in my classroom hangs a sign:

*Thru this door walk big, tuff guys who love football.*

The importance of tuffness is affirmed with my players every time they walk through the classroom door. If they aren't tuff, then they won't be walking through my door for very long. In many ways, the survival of the fittest is the survival of the tuffest.

I have one further thought regarding tuffness:

*Football is a tuff game, played by tuff people …. It's coached by people who aren't as tuff as they think they are.*

> **Tuff** is the way this football coach likes to spell tough. To my eyes, the word *tough* doesn't even look *tuff!*

# Tensed - Relaxation

There is a balance between being too tight and too relaxed with all forms of physical performance. Some skilled quarterbacks can throw the short dump pass with firm control, while others either float the ball or drill it to the receiver. We typically refer to the skilled quarterback as having "touch".

As a boy, I remember going to see Cincinnati Reds [*should be*] Hall of Famer Pete Rose at an autograph event. I remember Pete talking about the importance of a stiff grip on the bat so that the batter could strike the ball hard. Charlie Hustle, as he was known, was my childhood hero and his pictures covered my bedroom walls. From that moment on, I gripped the bat firmly with a strong grip. It wasn't a death grip; but, it certainly wasn't a loose or medium strength grip, either. I later discovered that I was successful when my grip was strong; but, my body was relaxed. I refer to this state as **tensed – relaxation**.

Similarly, some skilled musicians are able to play softly (pianissimo) while the entire, large audience hears the music clearly. Unfortunately, other musicians are unable to play soft music in a large setting. Albert refers to this technique as playing **Loud – Soft**. If a musician can play soft tones that carry over the hushed roar of an audience, he is able to "project". [*pro•ject not proj•ekt*] For a gentle song to project, the singer should visualize that he is singing softly to the farthest person in the back row of the audience.

Playing the piano requires a solid grip on the keys with the fingertips. As Albert explained to me, the fingers are flexed and rigid and the power is generated through the shoulders and arms as the hands pivot to center the force. The weight of the arms should feel as though they have "follow through" beyond the fingertips on the keys. The typical piano "grip," in Albert's opinion, has a similar feeling to carrying a light suitcase; the work is done with the arms and upper body, while the fingers keep tension on the handle.

In football, the best hits are made when a player hits through an opponent. Football coaches like to say:

"Hit through, not to."

"Aim beyond the target."

Usually when a football player tries to hit his opponent really hard, he is rarely successful. Trying to deliver the "crushing" blow, typically results in bodily tension and limits the player's ability to generate force. From observing martial arts, championship power lifting and professional football, I have affirmed that:

*More power comes from relaxed muscles than clenched teeth.*
*[Repetition is the mother of learning.]*

---

Firm grips can encourage tightness. The elite tennis player learns to grip firmly without tightening his forearm in order to increase his stroke velocity and to prevent tennis elbow. The professional trumpet player develops a firm grip with his lips without straining his jaw and cheek muscles. [ By the way, *is he rightfully a **trumpetist** as is: a violinist, a trombonist, a percussionist, an oboist, a cellist, a flutist, a bassoonist, a saxophonist, a timpanist or a guitarist?*] The skillful pitcher grips the baseball with a firm grip while he relaxes his wrist, arm and shoulder.

Ultimately, all elite physical performance requires both firm, controlled tension and muscular acceleration with follow through. Anyone who has played sports has heard his coach address the importance of a good grip, follow through and relaxation. I suggest that all physical movements are maximized when there is firm tension at the contact spots and muscular relaxation throughout the remainder of the body. Both tension and relaxation are required simultaneously! In order to generate explosive movements, tensed - relaxation is required.

> "Tension is who you think you should be.
> Relaxation is who you really are."
> **Chinese proverb**

# Bridges and Arcs

Have you ever stopped to look at a suspension bridge and wondered why it has an arched shape. Why it isn't completely level and flat?

Have you ever looked at ancient Roman architecture and observed the arches built into the open spaces .... the doors, columns and the windows?

Have you ever observed the flight of powerful airborne objects whether it's an airplane in take off, a driving golf ball, or a batted homerun ball and noticed why they fly outwardly (horizontal) as they climb (vertical) into the air?

A few years ago, my wife and I were touring the Fort at Old San Juan in Puerto Rico. Fort San Felipe del Morro was built in the 16th Century as a military installation to protect the entrance from pirate and enemy ships into the San Juan Bay and the city of Old San Juan. From the fort, which was situated high on a bluff, the soldiers would fire cannons at the ships from the fort's cannon rooms. The cannon rooms were oddly shaped with arched ceilings.

"Why the arched ceilings?" my wife asked.

"The arched room is able to withstand the tremendous power from the cannon fire better than a square room," I replied in a confident, matter-of-fact tone. [I had just read the placard explanation outside of the cannon room.] *Arcs and Arches*.

In biomechanics, we refer to forces as being either linear or angular. The movements of bodies are recognized as having either linear momentum or angular momentum. **Angular momentum** is the secret to developing power.

Previously, we acknowledged the importance of a solid grip at the contact spots with relaxed muscles between the points. Think again of that suspension bridge. It is anchored firmly into the banks on both ends and the remainder of the bridge is flexible; it is able to sway and withstand the forces of the wind and the over passing cars.

Albert once told me that he thinks of his piano posture (stance) as a suspension bridge. He is anchored with his butt on the bench and his fingertips on the keys. Between those two points, his entire body is relaxed and flexible. From that stance, he is able to exert angular power from his upper body through his hands and into the keys. Sometimes when a pianist has to play especially forceful, he will anchor his feet into the ground so that he is able to use the power from his legs and hips through his body chain to the keys.

While playing, Albert thinks of moving his hands in circles. Just as an elite violinist moves the bow in swaying, circular motions, the pianist does the same. The pianist is able to exert more power into the keys by adding some angular (circular) movement to the hands and arms rather than striking the keys like pistons in an up and down motion. If you would like to see this circular technique in action, watch a YouTube video of the Astonian pianist, Valintina Lisitsa. *Her sound is breathtaking.*

Willie played football with a tremendous power base. He had the ability to bend his knees and play with his feet spread apart. Years ago, I attended Willie's pro tryout day at Auburn University. I asked Willie to extend his arms in front of himself as I grabbed his wrists with my hands. I tried to push his arms downward, towards the ground, to gauge his strength. They didn't budge. *I could have done chin-ups on his outstretched arms.* I was awed by his strength and the stability of his base.

Willie was more than a brute. He was an excellent athlete with quickness, balance and coordinated control. Because of his strong base, he was able to anchor and accelerate his athletic body to generate explosive power.

Over ten years ago, John Green, a sales representative for Rogers Athletic Company, approached me. Rogers makes football sleds...large hunks of metal that football players push around to develop their leg strength and their blocking techniques. Driving these massive machines requires exhaustive effort from the players; blockers typically hate pushing sleds around the football field. John wanted to know my general thoughts regarding blocking sleds.

"They can build bad habits," I explained to John. "Sleds can encourage players to fire out of their stances quickly and they are good for conditioning. But they don't mimic blocking accurately."

All blocking sleds, at that time, were designed in a way that the blocker either fired straight ahead or that he lifted up immediately after contacting the sled. Blocking is a combination of both. Blockers fire out flat and then transition to an arching, upward movement as they recruit the large muscles in the legs, hips and back. The hands and the feet are the anchor points while the flexible body exerts the angular momentum in a snapping motion to create acceleration.

John replied, "Let's design a sled that mimics blocking."

John, the guys at Rogers and I undertook a mission to design a sled that would change the industry. The **Lev Sled**™ was developed to train the correct movements of blocking technique by incorporating three dimensional skills and angular momentum. The Lev Sled has become the industry standard and the most popular blocking sled in the field. I take great satisfaction knowing that I have helped to provide a miserable experience for thousands of football players in their quest for improving their blocking techniques and their conditioning. No lineman has ever thanked me for my contribution; many have cursed my existence.

Angular movements help create acceleration rather than linear force. You can find inspiring examples of angular motions in all elite physical performances. Sports skills that involve kicking, throwing, spinning, hitting, lifting, serving, thrusting or twisting all require arched movement patterns. It's the difference between a "stiff" performance and a "fluid" performance.

> "Kites rise highest against the wind than with it"
> **Winston Churchill**

# "Education 101 – Teachers Eyes in the Sun"

During my undergraduate studies in Physical Education at SUNY Cortland, we were taught that the teacher/coach should always face the sun when addressing the students. Dr. Snell mentioned it one day as an aside, but it should be written in a textbook! [*I guess now it has!*] What seems like common sense must be most uncommon. Sometimes, the closest some people get to common sense is when they reach in their pockets.

Have you ever wondered why your kid is looking down at the ground for clovers when the coach is speaking to the team?

The natural human response is to avoid the bright sun by turning away from it. The unskilled coach will gather the team together for instruction with his back still to the sun. Since the athletes are positioned facing the sun, they respond by shielding their eyes [*for a while*] or look down at the ground. I require my athletes to look at my eyes when I am talking to them. Standing with my eyes facing the sun makes it a lot easier for the players to focus on me.

One night, while searching Google images for photos, I found 30 images of athletes looking into the sun before I stumbled upon my first photo of the coach facing the sun. *Amazing.* When I call my players together for instruction, I always find the sun and position myself accordingly.

Sometimes other distractions take precedence over sunlight. One summer, as I was coaching one of my high school football camps, I was informed that the cheerleader camp was running concurrently. In fact, they were practicing on the adjacent field to ours! Guess which direction we ran our drills?

Ultimately, the coach should see through the eyes of the performer.

"The sun illuminates only the eye of a man, but shines into the eye and the heart of the child"
**Ralph Waldo Emerson**

# SLOW DOWN

Albert walked to the opposite side of the classroom, sat down and said:

"Play for me..."

I had been working on "Für Elise" for over a month. It was my third bi-weekly lesson on the piece. I was starting to play it in the rhythm and the tempo (speed) that was required. The notes were mostly right with the exception of an occasional mistake. After playing through the piece, I sat waiting for Albert's critique.

"How do you feel about it?" Albert asked

"I hate it," I gruffly replied. "It sounds too mechanical. I can't make it sound expressive like you can."

"It's because you practice it too fast." Albert offered, "For the next two weeks I don't want you to practice it faster than half speed. Not once. Most of the times I want you to practice it as slowly as you can stand."

Practicing slowly ensured that there were no extraneous movements in the fingers and hands as they found their way to the next keys. By practicing slowly, I had to mentally direct my fingers and hands.

"I'm a general. My soldiers are the keys, and I have to command them." I recalled reading the quote from Vladimir Horowitz.

Secondly, slow motion practice allows the pianist to control the weight and strike of the keys, which affects the note's texture. If he can't play expressively in slow motion, it is impossible to generate expressive sound at full speed tempo.

"Try to make each note sound differently than the note before," Albert instructed. "Also, every time the melody returns, it must sound uniquely different. Otherwise it's boring."

As an obedient student, I followed Albert's instructions. For two weeks, I did not play faster than half speed. This required self-control because *it killed me*. I could only taste the batter; but, I wanted to taste the cake that I was baking.

Sergei Rachmaninoff, the early 20th Century composer, was also a virtuoso pianist. He was once observed rehearsing for a performance of Chopin's "Etude in Thirds". This particular Etude is a difficult piece and is performed very fast with the hands flying up and down the keyboard. What was unusual, however, was that Rachmaninoff was practicing the piece at a super slow motion tempo, maybe five seconds between each chord.

In football, we do a lot of walk through practices for teaching and repetition purposes without the physical grind of full speed practice. I teach football techniques that are even slower than that. I call it my **super slow motion tempo**. I want the mind to control the movements from preparation to execution. Slow speed rehearsal can develop muscle memory more quickly than rehearsing at full speed while making errors. Slow speed rehearsal also eliminates all extraneous transitional movements. I've found the most consistent linemen can step through techniques slowly with balance and purpose. Blockers who are unable to perform a technique correctly at super slow motion tempo are usually "feel" players. Feel players are typically inconsistent.

"Prepare," Albert would implore while practicing.

Before the fingers leave the keys, the pianist knows exactly where they are going next. You don't move your hands after playing notes and then find where to place them. As the hands are moving, they are feeling the fingers lock into the position that will grab the keys.

"Hold the keys," Albert would insist.

Before playing the key, the pianist actually has made physical contact with the keys. A full, warm tone is accomplished by the entire weight of the hand, arms and shoulders falling through the keys that are already held. A shrill, hollow tone is produced when the keys are struck sharply without control.

Two weeks later, I played "Für Elise" for Albert at half speed. This time there was expression. The notes had individual texture and character and the phrases flowed with purpose. The dynamics (volume) varied throughout the work.

"Ok, now play it at regular tempo for me," Albert suggested.

*It worked.*

After two weeks of uninspired, slow motion rehearsal, the muscle memory was established. The full speed performance had the same expression as the half speed performance.

Athletes and musicians should practice their mechanics in a slow, focused manner. My advice to all learners of physical performance is to not be in a hurry when learning a new skill. Create the proper muscle memory and the neural pathways of the correct execution. By using slow, intense repetition, you will be more proficient with the skill than by racing through the learning period. It's easier to speed up good habits than to break and retrain poor habits.

> "The two most powerful warriors are patience and time."
> **Leo Tolstoy**

# Pounded Movements

When a performer learns a new skill pattern, he should practice it decisively and with tremendous energy, strength and control. This is true of movements that require power, as well as movements that require finesse. Too often, finesse movements become lackadaisical and lose their energy. By **pounding movements**, the learner develops the muscle memory in intense, bright execution.

While training, a football player will emphasize proper footwork by driving his foot into the ground forcefully. This overemphasis builds strong, decisive muscle memory. The same is true of the actor who overemphasizes his diction or the singer who cleanly separates his notes in a rehearsed arpeggio. A pianist develops the talent of playing smooth, legato scale passages by initially playing each note independently with attention to its individual, unique texture and timing.

*Here's the important key to it all:*

After practicing in slow motion, with pounded movements, the performer then should replicate the movement patterns faster. Not with more force, effort or change in balance... just faster.

> "Might makes Right"
> **Plato**

# Towel Drill

Great physical performers possess **kinesthetic awareness**, meaning that they need neither their eyes nor their ears to place their bodies in the right positions. Their **muscle memory** aids in the awareness of knowing their body position as it relates with space. Divers and gymnasts, in particular, require a keen sense of kinesthetic awareness. An athlete who possesses great kinesthetic awareness is like a compass that always points north. Kinesthesia is a sixth human sense.

Occasionally, I use blind footwork drills with my offensive linemen by placing a towel over their heads. First, the blocker performs a skill with his eyes open. Next, he will put a towel over his head and try to replicate the same skill. I will video this drill so that the blocker can judge his mastery. I have found that my most consistent game performers are also the best performers in this blind drill. Kinesthetic awareness is a talent just like running fast or jumping high.

Sometimes offensive linemen are required to block without audio cues. Usually the lineman moves when he is commanded by the quarterback's cadence; the cadence provides the blocker the advantage of initiating the first movement versus his opponent. In a loud stadium, the offensive football players cannot hear the QB bark his commands over the roar of the crowd. Even when Willie had to block a defender who was lined up to his outside, he would oftentimes have to look to his inside at the ball and react after it was snapped. Looking at the ball requires the blocker to approach his defender blindly. Blocking a defender with your vision displaced, even momentarily, requires confidence and kinesthetic awareness. The towel drill helps to train kinesthesia.

Jerry Sullivan, a long time top NFL wide receivers coach, would train his receivers to run pass routes while they wore painted sunglasses. Painted sunglasses effectively rendered the player blind. Sullivan believed that a receiver could never really know how far a 15 yard route was until he felt the timing in his body without the measured cues from his eyes.

Pianists sometimes rehearse their memorized music wearing a blindfold, their hands covered up or their eyes closed. The muscle memory and feel of the keys with the fingers is a higher level of performance than responding mechanically from visual cues. It's amazing to watch the great musicians perform solos expressively with their eyes closed. It's just as amazing watching a musician perform as he is reading the music score and not looking at his hands. Both performers have developed skills of kinesthesia.

The reader begs the question:

"How do they do it? How does a pianist make blind, rapid, skips?"

*It looks almost impossible.*

The answer:

"He trains with slow, pounded movements. He breaks the music into small parts and rehearses the measures perfectly over and over again. He closes his eyes as he feels his body interact with space."

The reader replies:

"I knew that."

Performing musicians sometimes have to overcome what they hear. *Stage performance never sounds like the practice room.* Novice performers can be startled by hearing the weaker tones come from their instrument or voice during performance on the vast stage. The musician's natural response is to play too loudly which ruins the musical expression. Stage musicians must trust that their music is projecting to the audience by the physical feelings [muscle memory] they have developed in their fingers, lips, vocal chords and nasal cavities.

Athletes profess that games are different than practice. It is faster and more unpredictable. Sometimes athletes don't find practice to be meaningful. But, practice is where technical habits are developed. By polishing his habits through practice repetition, the performing athlete is able to trust that his technique will help him overcome the rigors of the game.

Muscle memory becomes stronger if the skill is learned correctly from the outset. With the knowledge of slow motion learning, and its effects on muscle memory, I have incorporated the concepts into my daily life. For example, whenever I get a new computer, I invest some time rehearsing my finger strokes on the keys that are invariably located in different spots than my last computer. If I fumble around from the beginning, and I continue to repeat this habit, then I never become proficient with that keyboard. All physical performers should develop correct muscle memory of kinesthesia from the beginning.

> "My eyes make pictures when they are shut."
> **Samuel Taylor Coleridge**

# The Alexander Technique

Frederick Matthias Alexander (1869-1955), an Australian Shakespearian actor, was losing his voice and his ability to project his lines. Since performance microphones weren't invented during his time, he was on the verge of a career change. He developed a series of techniques that relaxed and optimized the muscles in his throat, face and torso so that he could produce vocal volume. His technique is simply referred to as **The Alexander Technique**.

Musicians have embraced his principles and have applied them to performance. Virtually every conservatory offers courses and some exposure to the Alexander Technique. One application as it applies to a string player (violin, viola, cello and double bass) is the mental image of the bow being pulled by a force outside of the performer.

> Instead of the performer using his muscles to push and pull the bow across the strings, the musician should feel as if someone has tied a rope to his arm and the rope is pulling his arm and his bow.

This mental image causes the recruitment of more muscles into the stroke. Greater muscle recruitment produces a fuller, more beautiful sound.

My players, who usually enjoy my musical and other non-football analogies, might be the first football players to ever to learn The Alexander Technique. Bobbie Williams was our longtime starter and a stellar performer, but had trouble moving quickly to his left from a right-handed stance. The harder and more emphatically he would step, the slower he would ultimately move. The Alexander Technique really helped him. The mental thought of some external force moving his leg for him, rather than Bobbie moving it himself, worked for him.

> "Tis skill, not strength, that governs the ship"
> **Thomas Fuller**

The technique especially helps with the feeling of follow through. Unfortunately, I'm related to F. Matthias Alexander about as much as I'm related to Alexander the Great and Brandy Alexander.

# Creative Practice

Developing solid muscle memory should be the first stage in learning a new skill. The elite performer is able to express those skills with confidence. To develop confidence, I recommend that the performer uses some deviant practice behavior once the skill is mostly learned.

Teodor Leschetizky (1830-1915) was a Polish pianist and professor of piano. He was a student of Carl Czerny, who was Beethoven's student. Leschetizky was a co-founder of the St. Petersburg Conservatory and was a famous teacher. Artur Schnable, one of the greatest Beethoven interpereters, was a student of Leschetizky. Among the array of Leschetizky's techniques, he recommended that his students practice their music backwards. (e.g., the student performs the last measure of the piece, then the last two, then the last three etc.)

I've tried practicing music backwards and have found it especially helpful when memorizing music. Albert has also encouraged me to practice music: too loud, too soft, too fast, too slow, too pompous, too shy, too happy, too sad and any type of creative way possible. Sometimes I will even play every third measure. Othertimes I will play the measures backwards from the end of the measure to the beginning of the measure (retrograde). More talented pianists can play the music lines upside down (inverted) or backwards and upside down (retrograde inversion). All of these tricks help the musician gain confidence, understanding and memorization of his music.

Since 1983, I have taught a particular blocking progression backwards (retrograde). Blocks are typically broken down into three phases: the approach, the transition and the finish. I teach the last element, the finish, first. By teaching the progression in reverse order, the confidence of the block seemingly increases from beginning to end. By practicing skills in retrograde progression, the performer develops a deeper understanding of the skill.

I use a series of blocking drills that we perform routinely. Prior to every practice, the players perform a footwork circuit that includes the array of techniques an offensive lineman must execute. The circuit drill prepares the player for a clean, technically focused mindset prior to practice. I've shared this drill with coaches at clinics, throughout the years, and it has become popular. To see the circuit drill, go to *www.perform-coach.com*. Perhaps, you can modify my drill to suit the technical requirements of your skill

Mundane drills for developing discipline and precision are important. But, you can't practice the same skills, the same way all of the time. Often times, the best drills are created on the spot in response to a specific performance error. Practice variance helps the performer develop a keener understanding of the skill.

> "Man's mind, once stretched by a new idea,
> never regains its original dimensions"
> **Oliver Wendell Holmes Jr.**

# Pedagogy

Coaches are teachers. Earlier I shared the analogy that teachers *are like painters*. Before the first brush stroke touches the canvas, the picture is already painted in their minds. Sometimes a high school coach is concerned that the "pro" techniques are too advanced for high school kids.

Over twenty years ago, my friend Norm Eash and I initiated the nation's first football camp (Midwest Linemen Camp) exclusively for linemen. Since the camp's inception, I have taught over 10,000 high school kids how to perform "pro" style blocking techniques. Remarkably, the kids learn these techniques easily. Pro techniques are usually quite refined; they are reduced to their simplest factors. Coaches can teach anything that they can understand and see clearly in their minds.

My first NFL coaching position was for the New York Jets in 1992. I arrived in New York with ten years of college coaching experience but was blown away by the knowledge, detail and skill of the professional coaching staff. I learned more tactical football during my first two months on the job than in any previous five year period. *At first, I felt overwhelmed with the NFL.* I wasn't confident of surviving my first twenty days, much less being able to enjoy my vocation of the past 20 years.

Bruce Coslet, the head coach of the New York Jets, hired me as an assistant coach in 1992. Watching Bruce teach a play to the team in the classroom was breathtaking. Bruce, a master wordsmith, could articulate pictures vividly. When talking about game situations, he clearly staged the environment so that you sensed that you were actually at the game as he spoke. Bruce didn't teach plays; he taught football. Bruce was a skilled performer.

Every football technique that I teach, I can physically perform myself. Before observing the performance of a skill, I know what it should look and feel like. Consequently, I can experience with my own eyes and body the performer's technique. A good skill is to use *photocognition* techniques to record the performer's event and then be able to mimic their techniques for them. Some performers learn most quickly from seeing what they are doing and then observing how a skill should be performed properly.

*It's not what is taught that matters, it's what is learned.*
Pavlo Sasha

My mother was a high school teacher and guidance counselor for 30 years. I grew up like the cobbler's son; I learned my trade at my Mother's apron strings. Mom loves teaching and learning. She still takes courses, volunteers at the library and reads voraciously. She has thousands of 3x5 cards filled with reviews of the books she has read. [She's also read and proofed this book a couple of times; if you find any grammatical errors, then take it up with Mom.]

The best piece of advice about teaching I received was from my mother. Mom insisted:

"Don't smile until Thanksgiving."

Good advice. The young teacher who starts off the first day like he is the student's friend is just setting the tone for the inevitable anarchy. Little effective learning takes place in chaos.

Mom tried to discourage me from being a teacher. In the late 1970's, there were very few teaching jobs available. Furthermore, she warned:

"You're not going to want to play around in the gym when you're 50 old."

I recalled Mom's warning on my 50th birthday. I still like playing around in the gym, the weight room and the football field like I did 30 years ago. I especially enjoy the personal relationships with my players as I watch them grow and learn. I inherited that joy from my Mom, always the teacher.

*Grownups can change. If grownups didn't change, why would we have clergy?*

I remember Dr. John Snell teaching us these axioms in an Education Methods course 30 years ago when I was an undergraduate student at SUNY Cortland:

"You can't send them all to the principal's office." [*The office isn't big enough.*]

"There will always be a problem student to assume that role in the classroom." [*The moment you eliminate the problem student, another will emerge.*]

Some of my friends, who are school administrators, have expressed that their best teachers rarely send their problems to the office. The best teachers handle their own problems. So do the best coaches.

My wife Kathy is a teacher. I call her Red. At this point you shouldn't find it surprising that my strong admiration for teachers led me to marry one. She was an Elementary English Major specializing in children's literature. We have the ongoing debate:

"Was your college course on nursery rhymes more difficult than my tennis class?"

It's probably a tossup. But, we both chose to follow our passions. Red took a leave from teaching when our three daughters were born. Given the crazy hours that football coaches work, I'm glad my kids are being raised by a teacher

Red is a master of the "Tom Sawyer Method". If Kathy had a wall to white wash, her friends would all grab a brush while she made the lemonade. She would do the same for them. [*But she would still make the lemonade.*] Her selfless generosity is contagious. I don't know how she does it; it just happens. I call her methodology a **chia pet** phenomenon. [*How do they grow so fast?*] Red is too soft to be a football coach, but a great teacher, nonetheless.

Great teachers come in different forms. Some are loud and threatening, while others are quiet and encouraging. In my view, the best teachers are true to themselves.

When setting the parameters for this book, I decided that I would not write about any current NFL coaches. I didn't want to compromise our professional relationships. I recognize, however, that many coaches are reading this book and that coaches love inspiring quotes. They especially enjoy the rhetoric of other coaches. I'm compelled to share these two great quotes:

"I see better than I hear."
Marvin Lewis

"He who defends everything, defends nothing."
Dick Le Beau

*The best coaches are the best teachers.*

"The more wit, the less courage."
**Thomas Fuller**

# Go in Peace

Catholics are usually good time managers.

I like to go to mass early so that I can get a good parking spot. The best parking spaces are directed facing the exit lane; many Catholics take great pride in parking their cars backwards to facilitate their quick escape. We go to mass, we say our prayers, we make our offerings, we participate in our sacraments and then we leave. In fact, at the conclusion of the mass, the priest's final command is:

"The mass is ended. Go in peace!"

In my family, we have a communication problem. When our mass has ended …. we stand around and talk! I've tried to tell my wife and her friends that we aren't Protestants. We don't "do" coffee, donuts and fellowship. When our mass is ended, we GO in peace. You can imagine my sullenness as I walk out to the parking lot and discover the irony of our perfectly parked car sitting mostly alone in a mostly empty parking lot.

When one of my nephews was in sixth grade (I better not say which one), he played on an All-Star lacrosse team. The team was organized to compete in a tournament against other out of town elite teams. They had six practices to prepare.

I attended the second practice. I witnessed 15 minutes of warm-ups, stretching and calisthenics followed by a fifteen minute skill period. For the next 90 minutes [*that's an hour and a half*] the kids stood in front of the coach as he lectured them on the finer points of lacrosse. *I was blown away*. In fact, I was told that the first practice followed the same format. In four hours of elite sixth grade lacrosse practice, the kids participated in lacrosse activities for a total of 30 minutes. *Wow!*

The story gets worse. At the end of the miserable practice, the coach huddled the boys together and proceeded to extend his talk for ten additional minutes. Finally, they mustered a lackluster cheer. The boys dragged their lacrosse sticks off the field, as if they were survivors of a death march.

In the tournament, I painfully watched his team's embarrassment. The first game ended 15-0; but, the dominance was worse than the score. We were held to two attempted shots on goal. After the game, the kids sat around a circle for 20 minutes as the coach analyzed the game. The team was dejected; the parents were despondent; and, I, as a member of the coaching profession, was infuriated. My guess is that the other teams didn't spend most of their time talking about lacrosse; they actually practiced lacrosse.

When I coach adult men, I never "lecture" on the

field for more than a few minutes. The attention span of even a focused learner is brief. Some coaches just like to hear themselves talk. Skilled coaches are able to express themselves with an organized and pointed economy of words.

To plan a practice properly, a coach should schedule more activity than the time permits. For example, a youth coach who plans a 60 minute practice should map out enough activities for 90 minutes of practice. The great youth coaches are able to transition quickly from drill to drill before their young athletes lose interest.

I've never understood why some coaches can't tell time. I surely speak for millions of parents who would like to share this message with their children's coaches, teachers and directors:

*Make sure the practice or rehearsal starts on time and ends when you say it will.*

I'm a blue collar worker by nature. I like to work hard, but when the horn blows ... I'm done. I coach the same way. I rarely find the need to lecture my players directly after a practice that I spent two hours coaching them. When our practice is over, we GO in peace.

# Down the Hall

I find this scene awkwardly comical.

In the school hallway, the athlete sees his coach walking towards him at the end of a long corridor. They are the only two people in the hall, and they are too far away to greet each other. *PANIC.* Both the athlete and the coach immediately look to the ground pretending that they don't see each other. Then, when they are five feet apart, they both look up acting surprised to see each other, and say "hello."

I know you've been there. The same situation often happens at work with co-workers. You've done it. You've participated in the fraud.

The next time you are in this situation, don't look away. Stare right at the person and start the conversation from 30 feet apart. Then chuckle to yourself after the two of you pass by. Enjoy the moment and the person's stunned expression. His expression typically turns into a smile.

Here's another expression-getter.

Many times I pass a player in the hall and he respectfully says:

"Hello Coach."

I like to reply:

"Hello Player."

Usually we both chuckle as we pass by.

> "Behavior is the image in which everyone
> shows their image"
> **Goethe**

# Third Person

Non-performers don't understand why some performers refer to themselves in the third person. Some find it silly while others may suggest schizophrenia. I muse at the quote from Terrell Owens (T.O.), the All Pro wide receiver.

"I'm going to work with T.O., and only T.O.," said T.O.

I understand it. Most focused performers see a third person as a standard for themselves. That fictitious **third person** might be an aggressive, clutch performer with nerves of steel. He is the very best performer of his craft in the business. Usually that third person is flawless and never makes error.

The focused performer is infused with energy when he strives to emulate the standard of the *fictitious third person*. If you don't believe it, watch the next time a performer makes a mistake, a penalty, a dropped ball or a swing and a miss. *"Whom is he talking to under his breath?"*

In the locker room prior to games, I've observed an amusing ritual. Many football players will dress into their game uniforms and then stare at themselves in the mirror. You can watch their game faces emerge as they confront their third person character eye-to-eye. Sometimes you'll see these warriors walk by the mirror in the bathroom quickly; but inevitably, many will turn and glance at the mirror as they affirm their character.

Most performers, thankfully, do not reference their third person character in public, lest everyone think they're nuts. But it's real.

I'm often asked, "How do you coach those *prima donna* millionaires? Actually, I coach primo uomini millionaires ..... The males with the lead roles in operas. [*Definitely not prima donna*s] Why should they listen to you? "

It's an interesting question, a very interesting question indeed.

1. The typical personal makeup of the professional athlete is that he is driven to be the very best. A strong sense of personal pride is how he ascended to the professional level in the first place and it accounts for his competitive personality.

2. If a professional athlete believes that the coach knows what he's doing, and that he can help the athlete improve his performance, he will do whatever the coach recommends.

3. The professional athlete must trust and believe that the coach will be fair and honest with him. The performer, however, must also understand that his personal

needs are subservient to the needs of the team.

4. Finally, I recommend to coach like the skilled wife coaches her elite performing husband ....... by nagging. Although the intentions of nagging vary, it seems to work. I like to joke with my players that the only reason I coach is so that I can tell someone else what to do. My married players can relate to that.

---

**nag·ging** [*from Coach Alexander's Dictionary*]
**1.** to encourage with positive intentions (fem.)
**2.** to nitpick in an irritating and demeaning way (masc)

---

If the coach is intimidated by the star or lacks expertise in his subject matter, the skilled performer can sense that vulnerability the way a shark smells blood in the water. I have seen NFL athletes virtually destroy an incompetent coach. Professional athletes don't always respect a coach simply because of his position of authority; they respect coaches who can help them achieve their goals and realize their dreams.

The successful professional coach wakes up every morning and makes the courageous, conscious decision to coach all the players, even if the great player has a diva personality. Sometimes the coach ends up with a headache because the player might resist criticism. Occasionally, the relationship between the coach and the skilled performer is a battle of wits, a survival of the fittest.

*Skilled coaches eagerly accept the responsibility of their responsibilities.*

> "It is so difficult to mix with artists!  You must choose businessmen to talk to because artists only talk about money"
> **Jean Sibelius (born 1889)**

# Cesar Millan

Cesar Millan is a professional dog trainer who is able to convert hostile, unmanageable dogs into docile, cooperative pets. Perhaps you've seen him on television or read his book, <u>Cesar's Way</u>, which should be required reading for all coaches and teachers. I've learned a great deal of practical human psychology from Millan's practical canine psychology. One of his fascinating observations is that dogs do not understand words; they only understand emotion that is projected from humans.

My friend, John, owns German Shepherds. He buys authentic Shepherds directly from Germany; they only understand German words. Hence, John trains his dogs with German commands since they don't understand English.

"Don't understand English?" I said to John. *I couldn't stop laughing.*

Teaching and coaching requires leadership. Humans are animals who also understand projected emotion. An effective leader is able to state his position by projecting convincing mannerisms.

My Dad was a good man. He was a hard working, dedicated family man who never had a pleasurable job. He worked in the Eastman Kodak Company factory while his shifts rotated from days to nights to afternoons. My Dad never complained; he was tuff. I never saw my Dad display weakness ... except when he watched the "Lassie" show on television. "Lassie" episodes caused my Dad to get emotional. My brothers and I used to laugh at him.

Dad didn't go to college, but he made sure that his sons did. My parents raised their four boys to be a group of achievers. My brothers and I were all Eagle scouts; we participated in sports and music/theater; and, we entered into professional careers. Dad was a creative thinker with a great sense of humor. We loved Dad, and we didn't ever want to disappoint him.

It was June of 2001 and we were visiting my parents. Dad was in the final stages of lung cancer and it was probably our last visit with him. During the trip, I caught a miserable cold. Since Dad's immune system was weak, I had to avoid contact with him.

Saying goodbye was hard. I remember the moment, as if it was yesterday, when I stood outside the front door and watched my wife and children hug my father for the last time. As he embraced them, he kept his eyes fixed on mine. His eyes spoke to me; he didn't need to say a word. From his comfortable, confident expression he promised me that everything was going to be ok and that his life was going to improve soon. We would be together again. He also told me that he was proud of me. Those unspoken words were delivered with perfect articulation. That comforting image returns to me regularly, especially when I seem to need it most.

*Effective communication is more than words.*

I was hired by Head Coach Dave Shula for the Bengals coaching staff in 1994. Dave Shula is the son of Hall of Fame Coach Don Shula, the winningest coach in NFL annals. I had only been employed a few months when Don Shula was visiting Cincinnati to play in his son's charity golf tournament. Dave, my boss, asked if I could chauffeur his dad. *Certainly, it would be an honor.*

After the golf outing, I proceeded to drive Don to Dave's house along a route that I had practiced; a route that worked. About half way home, Coach Don Shula ordered:

"You need to turn right here, right now."

Without hesitation, I quickly made the turn. An hour later, we were completely lost without the assistance of today's mobile phones or navigators. [*We were real men and we weren't going to stop for directions.*] Don's nonverbal cues suggested it was my fault that we were lost. Not only did I get the legendary Don Shula lost, I got my boss's Dad lost. Not good. Don reluctantly admitted:

"Well, I've only been to Dave's house a couple of times. You shouldn't have made that right turn."

*Yeah. No kidding.*

As I reflect on that awkward experience with a chuckle, I'm convinced that Don Shula was like the Pied Piper. He could lead. I didn't question him for a moment, even when he confidently instructed me to make the wrong turn. No wonder he could inspire and lead his team to so many victories.

My daughter, Mary Beth, is a student at Ohio State. She loves animals and science; for obvious reasons, she majors in Animal Science. She's always had the flare of Cesar Millan. Mary Beth could lead horses confidently when she was about eight years old. She can manage animals easily by her presence, the tone of her voice and the expressive confidence she exudes. For many years, Mary Beth couldn't decide if she wanted to be a Zoologist or a Biology teacher. In her case, communicating with animals and communicating with humans is *uno del stesso.*

Some leaders are verbose while others speak few words. Effective leaders possess confident emotional persuasion. The definition of leadership is the ability to inspire, the ability to convince.

> "We convince by our presence."
> **Walt Whitman**

# Performance Tests

[ **a parody** .... *Reminisce dei miei vecchi manuali di instruzione* ]

Athletes, musicians and actors possess talents that are specific to their art. Sometimes these skills come naturally to the performer; but, other times skills require development. Would you like to test your abilities as a natural pianist, football player or linguist?

**Polyrhythm** challenge:

1.  Try to clap four evenly spaced beats with your left hand on your left thigh while simultaneously clapping three evenly spaced beats with your right hand on your right thigh.

2.  Make sure both hands start and end at exactly the same time (but four beat for the same duration as three). Repeat the sequence repetitively without pauses.

3.  If you can do it, you can execute polyrhythm (multiple simultaneous rhythms). You can easily walk and chew gum at the same time. My guess is that you're either a drummer or a pianist. If you can't do it, you're like 99% of the rest of the population.

Polyrhythm is a skill for athletes as well as musicians. When an offensive lineman blocks a defender, his hands usually work independently of his feet. Some less skilled blockers are not able to keep a steady pace [rhythm] with their feet while adjusting their hands and body to the varied requirements of the situation.

**Carioca** challenge:

1.  Try to shuffle laterally, but cross your right foot in front of your left, and then spread your left foot completely.

2.  Cross your right foot behind your left. Extend. Stay low and do this repeatedly as fast as you can.

3.  If you can carioca, then you're either a football player or some type of movement specialist. If you fall down, then you too are like 99% of the rest of the population.

Carioca style techniques are used by the musician as well the athlete. A pianist must be able to cross his thumb underneath his other fingers rapidly and in rhythmic unity when playing scale passages. This difficult manipulation of the thumb is one of the main reasons why pianists spend so much time rehearsing scales.

**Linguist** challenge:

1.  My daughter's name is Mary Beth. Her boyfriend's last name is Seither.

2.  Try to bite and suck hard on a lemon and then immediately say Mary Beth Seither three times quickly without messing up.

3.  If you can do it, you're Mary Beth and I love you.

The linguist challenge has little direct application to the musician [*unless you're a singer*] or the athlete. It does highlight the importance of developing coordination, body control and discipline.

I became a better football player in college because as a Physical Education Major, I took skills courses in all sports: gymnastics, volleyball, basketball, dance, lacrosse, track and field, soccer etc. We call it "crossover training" in our field. The theory, and I believe it to be true, is that your body develops increased coordination, neuromuscular timing and strength by performing a variety of activities.

I'm always skeptical of an NFL prospect who played only football in high school. Virtually, all NFL players were two or three sport athletes in high school. If you're an athlete, a musician, an actor, a speaker, a teacher or a coach, then I recommend you vary your performance experiences as much as possible. When in doubt, perform. The greater the challenge, then the greater the potential gain.

*The only way to improve balance is to overcome being off balance.*

"Iron rusts from disuse, water loses it's purity from stagnation ... even so does stagnation sap the vigours of the mind."
**Leonardo da Vinci**

# SECOND OPINIONS

Have you ever had a kidney stone? I've had more than 30 of them. And I've been to numerous doctors and specialists. Unfortunately, they have all told me that the type of stone that I produce is incurable. "Drink lots of water," they say. That was until I met Dr. Caballero [*i.e. the horseman*].

"Cabby," as he's called, practices in Georgetown, Kentucky … the site of the Bengals summer training camp. Six years ago, I developed a nasty stone. At that time, I was experiencing them monthly; I was a "kidney stone producing machine," as Cabby phrased it. All of my stars were aligned perfectly for making stones. I was in the hospital as Cabby was making his rounds oddly in the middle of the night. [*He's a bit of the free spirited, eccentric type …. my kind of guy.*]

"That's ridiculous," snapped Cabby as he threw the metal medical chart across the room, waking up the patients nearby.

"They've known how to correct this stone for years…with crushed up lemon rinds."

Cabby prophesized, "You'll never have another stone."

My feelings were mixed because I thought this guy was nuts and I honestly didn't feel crushed up lemon rinds could do anything but freshen up the smell of a garbage disposal. Nonetheless, I've followed Cabby's advice and because of the lemon rinds (Uro CitK), I haven't had a kidney stone since. If you've ever had a stone, liked I posed at the outset, you'll know why I love Cabby.

The American College of Sports Medicine issued its official position paper in the late 1970's on the effects of anabolic steroids. I was a graduate student in Exercise Physiology; and, as a young scientist, I was convinced that science had all the answers. *Truth was only through data.*

The official professional position concluded that there was no evidence to indicate that steroids definitively caused an increase in muscular strength. Any *perceived* gains were likely either from water retention, which added to muscular bulk (hypertrophy) and possible psychological placebo effects.

"Are they crazy?" I asked my professor.

Unlike a research scientist, I was experienced in the world of athletics and knew the effects of taking steroids. They worked. The athletes experienced serious gains; the negative side effects were also extreme. [They are rightfully illegal as the physical effects are devastating.] After reading this position paper, I wondered if there were also position papers stored away on the positive results of blood leeching and the practice of withholding fluids to cure illness. Today, I think of poor Franz Schubert who might have died not from his syphilis, but from the mercury poison that the Doctors prescribed as medicine to cure his malady.

> Schubert's famous "Ave Maria" is actually "Ellens dritter Gesang" ("Ellen's Third Song). No one, *who is currently living*, knows who added the words of the Catholic "Hail Mary" prayer to Schubert's song.

Twenty years ago, I made a visit to an expert allergist to be evaluated. He asked me what I thought I might be allergic to, before he performed tests.

"Number one, I'm allergic to pine trees."

"That's impossible," said the specialist. "No one is allergic to pine trees. They don't produce enough pollen to cause a reaction. We don't even have tests for it."

*I left the office confused.* I thought I had finally figured out why I got a sinus infection every Christmas as a child and when camping as a Boy Scout. Oh, well. *Keep thinking.*

Ten years later, I returned to the specialist.

"You know Doc, I know you think it's impossible," I said, "but I'm pretty sure I'm allergic to pine trees."

"That's actually possible," the specialist had changed his tune. "Just recently studies have shown that some people are actually allergic to pine."

*Oh, really?!!. Grmmmmph!*

Why is this segment about medicine in a book on performance? Everyone, especially athletes, is confronted with medical issues. I firmly believe in seeking second medical opinions, and that's no indictment on any doctor. I believe that medicine, in many ways, is the ultimate profession of skepticism. The disciple Thomas [*"Doubting Thomas"*] should have been a doctor.

A doctor friend of mine and I recently had a discussion about a particular football situation. Of course, he knew all of the problems and he had all the solutions. Unfortunately, I have little tolerance for uniformed **expertism**. [*A new word*]

"You know doctors and coaches are a lot alike, but with one important difference," I quipped *omnisciently*.

Doc paused and asked, "Really, what's the difference?"

"*You* guys think *you're* God."

"Men give away nothing so liberally as advice."
**Francois de la Rochefoucauld**

# S.T.A.R.

Benjamin Leibowitz PhD is a psychologist who has spent his life studying coaching styles. Ben has analyzed the styles of hundreds of successful coaches including: Mike Ditka, Marv Levy, Bobby Bowden, Kurt Ferentz, Nick Saban, Joe Paterno, Bo Schembechler, Don James and Tom Osborne. [*He's also studied famous coaches from sports other than football*] After much research, he formulated four predominant coaching styles:

> **S.** earcher
> **T.** echnician
> **A.** nalyzer
> **R.** elater

All coaches, certainly have traits of each style, but the traits of each predominant style according to Ben are:

## Searcher
- imaginative, creative
- he values innovation
- he works most effectively in a flexible environment
- Bill Walsh would be an example of the Searcher Style.

### Technician

- pragmatic, results, stats, technique and execution
- he values effort
- he works most effectively in an organized environment
- Vince Lombardi would be an example of the Technician Style.

### Analyzer

- complex, objective
- he values ideas
- he works most effectively in a scientific environment
- Bill Belichek would be an example of the Analyzer Style.

### Relater

- personal motivation, loyalty, team work
- he values friendship and personal relationships
- he works most effectively in a positive environment
- Tony Dungy would be an example of the Analyzer Style

I met Ben close to 20 years ago in New York and was fascinated with his work. With his research, not only does Ben identify the styles, he proposes how to work with these coaches most effectively. Further research on Ben's writing, and an assessment tool for analyzing coaching styles, can be searched at: www.coachpsych.net.

After thinking about Ben's work, I've concluded that there is no mold for the "ideal coach". *This was a significant revelation to me.* I used to think the perfect line coach was a cut from the Technician Style, but I never felt comfortable playing that role. After taking the assessment, I realized that I drifted more towards the Analyzer Style. After noting several successful coaches with a similar profile to mine, I developed confidence that my style could work.

The "perfect" coach doesn't need to be tougher, or smarter, or get along better with his team, or run more imaginative plays, or work more on technique, or become more/less organized etc. I believe that it's most important for a coach to be himself and to know his strengths and weaknesses so well that he can make it work.

"You" just need to be the best "you."

> "God has given you one face and you make yourself another."
> **William Shakespeare**

# Positive Practice

Inevitably, a couple times every season, a coach makes the following statement within my ear's reach.

"That's why we practice," encouraged one coach after a player blew his assignment.

*"No that's why we meet, have walk throughs and playbooks,"* I grumbled under my breath.

My players know that I hate dismissing error too easily. I believe that all performers learn more from doing a skill properly, than by messing it up. Football, like most sports, is a game where the victor usually combines calculated dare with the fewest errors.

Jim McNally, a great friend and mentor, coached professional football for 28 years and really believed in positive practice reps. Before a segment of plays, Jim would gather his linemen and look at the plays versus the exact defense that they would encounter within the next few minutes. *Jim would cheat.* Most coaches prefer to practice offensive plays without knowledge of the impending defensive alignment … just like in a game.

"They learn more from doing it right than doing it wrong," Jim said.

Jim is the type of guy who is very positive and doesn't like confrontation with his players by yelling at them and pointing out all their errors in practice. Jim is also one of the best offensive line coaches in the history of the NFL; he has invented and inspired much of the contemporary offensive line techniques. If there were a hall of fame for assistant coaches, Jim would be a first ballot entry. Jim believed in manipulating practice for success. He also has a great sense of humor.

"You're going to feel miserable on Sundays during the game anyway," said Jim, "why be miserable on Wednesdays?"

Positive practices develop confidence. Players learn more by doing things right than by making mistakes. Practices still need to be challenging but not much is gained from a practice filled with mistakes.

> "If it weren't for the games, coaching would be the best job in the world."
> **Jim McNally**

# Achilles Heel Traits

If you can't hit the curve ball, you can't play Major League Baseball. [Unless you're an American League pitcher]

Professional coaches and athletes will eventually find an opponent's weakness, if they have one, and then they'll exploit it. I call those types of weaknesses **Achilles Heel Traits**. No matter how strong the armor is, a weakness if it is significant enough will be your undoing. I have a list of required traits – some physical, some mental and some competitive, that must be met at least adequately for me to recommend a potential player for our team. I believe that if a player fails in an area, then he will fail as a player.

Have you ever wondered why some athletes can have great rookie seasons and then never repeat that same success again? It's because the opponents figure them out. Somewhere they have an Achilles Heel Trait that gets exploited. They keep throwing curve balls.

Aaron Gibson, an offensive tackle from the University of Wisconsin, was a huge, flexible man and a 1st Round Draft Pick by the Detroit Lions in 1999. Everyone was impressed with Aaron's ability to do the splits like a gymnast, like an acrobat. It was freakish. Flexibility is a very important trait that an offensive lineman must possess. But, excessive flexibility is useless. The fact that his hips were double jointed had absolutely no positive application in football. The reason he failed was because he was too slow. Flexibility doesn't matter when you can't run fast enough to block your opponent.

Every performer who aspires to greatness, has to work on his weaknesses just as hard as he works on his strengths. Aaron should have spent more effort on his quickness than his flexibility. No one wants to focus on the areas that they're not good at. But, if a performer fails to strengthen his weaknesses, then he becomes exposed to the same fate as Achilles. In order to withstand the test of time, you must overcome your deficiencies.

> "I've stood upon the tomb of Achilles' and heard Troy doubted: time will doubt of Rome."
> **Lord Byron**

# "Kids these days..."

*"Children nowadays are tyrants. They contradict their parents, gobble their food and tyrannize their teachers."*
Socrates

In the 1970's, my generation of boys wore long hair. Our fathers couldn't understand why we wanted to look like girls. Perhaps we were *communists*, they thought.

"Where was Joe McCarthy when you needed him?"

> **Joe McCarthy** was a US Senator who led a witch hunt in the 1950's against politicians and prominent Americans whom he identified as potential communists and Soviet spies.

I remember hearing my teachers and other elders refer negatively to the "kids these days". "When I was a kid ........," [*We lived in Utopia, and had to walk to and from school uphill, and we respected our elders blah, blah, blah.*]. According to Socrates, this complaining has been going on for quite awhile.

In fact, my parents grew up in a generation where the older establishment viewed Elvis Presley as *"the devil on earth."* In 1957, Elvis was a guest on the Ed Sullivan show and they restricted the filming to above his waist. Many found his dancing and hip gyrations to be immoral. But, guess what .... my parent's generation, when they were kids, rebelled against their parents as they embraced rock and roll.

Today's generation of kids get tattoos and body piercings; maybe they're even a little "Goth". Their Rap music is no more offensive than Rock and Roll probably was to the parents of the 1950's. Maybe "Glee" is today's "Elvis". Kids basically want to grow up and experience life in a unique, exciting way. I think kids are great and their essence is the same as kids since the beginning of humanity.

Kids eventually blaze the trail for the rest of society to follow. In my lifetime, kids started wearing khakis (preppy), and then adults followed. The same happened with blue jeans, bell bottomed jeans and even baggy jeans. I'm sure that sometime in the near future, grandpa is going to be wearing his baggy jeans "down low" with his colorful boxers popping up. When that disturbing image is fulfilled, kids will quickly seek a new fashion statement.

Some of the older generation certainly jumped on the band wagon with rock and roll, longer hair and the current tattoo craze. At different moments in my life, I could not envision a senior citizen with a Walkman, a microwave, an iPod, a texting mobile phone or even a computer. In fact, tracking the trends of the youth is probably a good investment strategy.

When I was a graduate student in the 1982, computer technology was just beginning to reach the fad status. Dr. Paul Games, during his final Statistics lecture, warned our class:

"The technology revolution is building steam. This revolution is like a train, you need to jump aboard. Those who don't will either be left at the station or run over by its power. Jump aboard."

Dr. Games' advice, at the time, was both controversial and prophetic. Our professor was an elderly man, well into his 60's, with a futuristic vision that rivaled the young students in his class.

*Progress rarely reverts.*

*And .. kids these days are good.*

As I grow older, it's my pledge to not join the group of sour old curmudgeons who find excessive fault with today's kids. Won't you join me? As a coach, it's critical to your relationship with your upcoming performers. They are the future.

> *A tree that stops growing ... dies.*
> **Pavlo Sasha**

# CHERTOCK'S INVITATION

"I spoke with Michael Chertock today," I mentioned to Albert as we walked to the classroom for our lesson.

Albert stopped and looked puzzled. Michael Chertock is the principal pianist for the Cincinnati Symphony Orchestra as well as the Chair of the Piano Department at the Conservatory. Albert was curious why I had spoken with Chertock.

"He wants us to play together in a concert called Pianopalooza."

*Albert looked horrified.*

Albert knew that Pianopalooza was Cincinnati's most important piano event of the year. No amateurs were invited to perform. Selected faculty from the Conservatory's Piano Department who were professional concert pianists comprised the program. Like any great department, there was healthy competition among the faculty and Pianopalooza was the moment when they could put their best feet forward. Albert still had not spoken and he began to look ill.

"I told him that we would be happy to play. It would be fun."

At this point in the conversation, Albert was ill.

"Are you sure he said Pianopalooza?" a stunned Albert asked.

I replied, "Yes, Pianopalooza."

We walked the final two minutes to our classroom without speaking. You could cut the tension with a knife. I sensed that maybe I had gotten into something over my head, but I had committed to do it. Albert certainly wasn't nervous about his performance. He's performed on huge stages throughout the world. He knew that his student, however, was terrified to play in front of small groups. Pianopalooza. We were committed. *We were stuck.*

"We have a lot of work to do," Albert said as he unlocked the classroom door. I walked into the classroom and headed to the piano. Albert was flushed; *I was excited.*

Albert and I met later in the week at the Conservatory's library to select the music. We chose pieces that were not above my ability, but sounded really impressive. Albert chose the first piece, a medley of three folk songs transcribed by Tchaikovsky. They were harmonically complex in nature, and the pieces were harsh sounding. I liked his choice; I realized that If I missed a note, then Albert could easily cover it up in the accompaniment. *No one would notice.*

I joked with Albert, " the main reason concert pianists choose pieces that nobody knows is so that the audience doesn't recognize their mistakes."

Albert laughed, "That's our secret."

I chose the second piece, a Brahms Waltz that everybody knows. It's a sweet lullaby tune [*no not THE Brahms Lullaby*] and a quiet, moving piece. Why did I choose such a beautiful, popular tune? Well, please allow me get up onto my soapbox for a minute. [*After all it's my book!*]

**People like melodies they know**. Never was this more apparent than an evening Kathy and I spent with our friends, Amy and Michal, at the Cincinnati Symphony Orchestra. The first piece on the program was Rachmaninoff's Second Piano Concerto, which everyone in the audience knew. Even if you don't know the title, trust me, you would recognize the melodies. The long, lyrical melodies capture the emotions of any listener. They are so beautiful that they have become very popular in concert performances, movies and have even been pirated to make pop songs.

The second piece, after intermission, was Shostakovich's Fifth Symphony. It's a thorny atonal work, but nevertheless has great historical significance as it saved the Russian composer's life in the Stalin-led reign of terror in the 1930's. The piece reportedly depicted the gloom and horror of the Nazi occupation in Leningrad (St. Petersburg). Shostakovich's secret memoir, published after his death, indicates that the piece was actually about Stalin's tyranny against the Russian people. In just over a year at the height of the Great Purge, over a half a million people were shot while another seven million were sent to the Gulag (concentration camps). Nonetheless, I think Shostakovich's mom was the only one who could hum this tune.

The audience jumped to its feet in ovation after the Rachmaninoff, but not the Shostakovich; although, both pieces were performed brilliantly. While the audience was humming along to Rachmaninoff, they were emotionally charged. As they listened to Shostakovich, they were just trying to figure it out. People enjoy melodies that are lyrical and familiar.

In college, I was the music leader of the folk group at our Newman Chapel on Campus. I always chose songs that the congregation knew. Perhaps we would insert a new song occasionally, but we would certainly repeat it until it became part of the repertoire. I would bet that no Catholic college congregation ever sang better or louder than ours did. Ever. In my cynical way, I think many church groups choose songs that the congregation won't recognize so that they can "perform" for them. Or they choose songs to "educate" them. In either case, I have a problem. Music is a glorious form of prayer. Frankly, the congregation can't pray gloriously while they are trying to sing and read the music and verse simultaneously. Such a skill is possessed by maybe one percent of those present in the congregation.

In all, our choice of music was good. We cleverly chose a piece that was difficult for the audience to detect mistakes. We also chose a beautiful piece that would be entertaining because the music was popular and lyrical. The audience would hum to it. They would enjoy it.

Albert insisted that I practice the pieces slowly and as loudly as I could play them. It was a large hall and he insisted that no one would hear the music unless we produced a big sound. I even learned how to play soft passages loudly. [*loud-soft*] You have to be a pianist to even begin to understand what that last metaphysical statement means.

"Do not move your hands until you know exactly where they are going."

"Know what the next chord or note feels like before placing your fingertips on the keys."

"Do not strike the keys until after the finger tips have already been placed in position."

Repetition of the music had to be meaningful as well.

"Practice different parts of the piece independently. Don't just always play from the beginning. If you get lost, you'll need to be able to jump back in someplace."

"Always stay in tempo. If a mistake is made, keep playing. Go back and correct your mistake later."

"Practice the music backwards." "Back and forth." "Forth and Back."

"Practice it too loud, too soft, too fast, too slow."

"Once you know the music, practice your skips with your eyes closed."

"Develop a feel for the keys, chords and lines."

Our expression would be important.

"Sing the melodies and try to make the piano sing like a violin and not a typewriter."

"Try to play each note with a different texture than the one before."

"Think of phrases, not notes."

There was much to work on and so many techniques to master. I found that Albert always offered the perfect coaching point at the right opportunity. The trick was to put it all together.

The week before the performance, we practiced together every day for an hour. We probably played the pieces over a 100 times together for our one shot at performance. We were going to be confident.

Early in the week, we nitpicked and decided exactly how we would perform each note. By midweek, Albert allowed no variation from the plan. By the end of the week, we knew the music and each other so well that we would make musical expressions. The music at that point was never played exactly the same way twice. That's how the performance, in reality, would be.

We had two dress rehearsals on stage with the exact piano on which we would perform. I pounded at that Steinway as we rehearsed.

Eventually, Steinway and I knew each other, and I was the boss. I could get him to sing exactly how I wanted.

Our final rehearsal, the day before the performance, Albert had a new trick up his sleeve. We went and practiced our routine on every piano on the first floor of the classroom wing. We tried one attempt only, on eight different instruments. Each piano felt unique; each seat height and location was slightly different. We were determined that nothing was going to bother us no matter how it felt on stage.

Finally, Albert told me to go home and practice in the suit that I would wear for the performance. The extra layers of clothing on my arms would feel differently than the short sleeved T-shirts that I typically wore. It was great advice.

I went home, tried to sleep and waited nervously.

# PERFORMANCE

*"It is not the critic who counts: not the man who points out how the strong man stumbles or where the doer of deeds could have done better. The credit belongs to the man who is actually in the arena, whose face is marred by dust and sweat and blood, who strives valiantly, who errs and comes up short again and again, because there is no effort without error or shortcoming, but who knows the great enthusiasms, the great devotions, who spends himself for a worthy cause; who, at the best, knows, in the end, the triumph of high achievement, and who, at the worst, if he fails, at least he fails while daring greatly, so that his place shall never be with those cold and timid souls who knew neither victory nor defeat."*

**Theodore Roosevelt**

# Brum

In November of 1991, the Baltimore Ravens were blowing us out in the third quarter. The Bengals had the ball and we called for our tackle counter play. Scott Brumfield, a huge offensive lineman from Brigham Young, was our right guard. He and the tight end collided helmets in the most unlikely fashion. Brum fell to the ground unconscious, paralyzed.

I remember running onto the visiting field, standing over him and looking at him in disbelief. At that moment, I was cast into the hardest acting role of my life. I looked intensely right at my guys; we shared the same intentions. *We would not fold.* Inside, however, I wanted to crumble.

Brum was rushed to the hospital as the game continued. With determination, we ran the ball over and over again. Huge holes. Touchdown! The game turned. Our emotional charge, in Brum's memory, resulted in overcoming a huge deficit to win the game.

I spent the evening with Brum and his wife, Jody, in the intensive care unit in Baltimore. The test results were grim. Brum was unconscious and there was a very real possibility that he would not come out of his slumber; at best, he would likely remain paralyzed.

Early the next morning, Brum regained consciousness. It took several hours for him to realize who he was, where he was and who we were. I remember his surprised, prideful expression when I told him he was an NFL football player and that I was his coach. He thought that was pretty impressive. As he became coherent, I was responsible to break the news to him. Somehow the words came out of my mouth.

"Brum, you're paralyzed."

Later in the day, Brum regained his mental faculties; but, he still couldn't move. I told Brum that I had to head back to Cincinnati to prepare for the next game. As I left the room with a tear in my eye, Brum said to me:

"Coach, I'll be back."

*The tear rolled down my cheek.*

"Brum, I just pray that someday you'll be able to play with your kids." I offered.

I left the hospital and flew back to Cincinnati with loneliness like I had never known. In the months that followed, I visited Brum often and I helped push him with every bit of coaching talent that I had. The doctors were convinced that he would never walk and run again.

In the end, because of Brum's great faith and his own hard work, he made a miraculous recovery. That next fall, Brum played right guard again for the Cincinnati Bengals. Today, Brum is the Head Football Coach at Dixie College.

*Why do we do this?*

Performers are wired oddly. They love what they do. The sacrifices and risks that an elite performer makes are not necessarily rational. Most elite performers have a close group of supporters who encourage his passion. Without the support and understanding from people in the performer's circle, he would be lost.

"Perpetual devotion to what a man calls his business is only to be sustained by perpetual neglect of many other things."
**Robert Louis Stevenson**

# Proverbs

[*Proverb .... a clichéd message*]

Mrs. Smith, the fifth grade teacher, told her class,

"Today we are going to share stories that end with a proverb. Who would like to go first?"

Sally started it off.

[**cantabile mesto** *...musical notation meaning:
to sing sadly.*]

"OK, so......One day my Dad took some of our hen's eggs from our farm to the chicken farmer. He loaded the truck and drove to the chicken farmer, but, on the way he hit a bump in the road and the all the eggs broke. He was very sad."

"Thank you for the story Sally," said Mrs. Smith. "What is the proverb?"

Sally replied "Don't count your chickens before they hatch."

"Very good Sally," said Mrs. Smith.

Suzie was next.

[**scherzo**... *the Italian translation is: a joke.
Scherzi are often played playfully, jokingly.*]

"OK, so......One day I was playing out in the yard and I tore my dress. Quickly, I ran in the house and my Mom put in a few quick stitches to mend the tear. I went back outside, but my dress tore worse."

"Thank you too for the story Suzie," said Mrs. Smith. "What is the proverb?"

Suzie replied, "A stitch in time saves nine."

"That's great Suzie," said Mrs. Smith.

Reluctantly, with a sigh, Mrs. Smith called on Johnny next.

*[apassionata... with emotional vigor, passion.]*

"OK, so......One day during the war my Dad was flying over the jungle when his plane got hit. Before it crashed, my Dad grabbed a case of beer, a machete and his machine gun then parachuted from the jet. His parachute got caught in a tree and he saw 1000 enemies approaching him. Immediately, he quickly drank the entire case of beer. With his machine gun, he shot the first 500 enemies. When he ran out of bullets, he grabbed his machete and then slashed the next 500 enemies' throats."

*[**sforzando**... sudden emphasis]*

"1000 enemies dead!"

"Oh my, Johnny, that's a horrible story!" gasped Mrs. Smith.

*[**fermata**... a long pause.]*

"What possibly could be the proverb?"

*[**marcato** ...each individual note is emphasized.]*

Johnny was convinced:

"Don't mess with my Dad when he's been drinking!"

That's the best joke I know. It's always guaranteed to provide a great response provided you do the following:

1. Instead of Johnny, use the boss's name, or someone else who the audience would like to laugh at.

2. Perform in the character of each person in the joke...sad Suzy, playful Sally and wacko

Johnny. Be sure to start each kid's story with "OK, so......" [*All kids do*].

3.  Always tell it with great passion, energy and rhythm where the verses transition into each other. Have moments that are piano, others that are forte. Incorporate rubato phrases and pauses, with accelerando and ritardando. Crescendo in order to inspire. Decrescendo to make them melt.

> *piano* softly played
> *forte* loudly played
> *rubato* a flexible tempo
> *accelerando* get faster
> *ritardando* slow down
> *crescendo* to get louder
> *decrescendo* to get softly

4.  If you are a lousy joke teller, try to tell this joke while incorporating the musical markings provided. After all, telling a joke is no different than a musical performance.

5.  Laugh. Smile and use great, awkward facial expressions. Laughter is like yawning; it's contagious. I don't tell any jokes that I don't think are funny. If the speaker is laughing, so will the audience. Guaranteed. Try it.

That joke reminds me of an experience I had with another literary term: *oxymoron.*

[*Oxymoron... contradictory terms*]

My high school was staffed by the Holy Cross Brothers and the Sisters of Mercy. My sophomore English teacher, Sr. Margaret Mary, was a Sister of Mercy. She taught us the meanings of numerous literary terms such as alliteration, personification, onomatopoeia and oxymoron.

While my family was visiting Washington, D.C. a few years ago, we visited the national monuments via a tour bus. Seated behind me were three pleasant middle aged women. After observing one of the ladies for several hours, my Catholic school instincts took over. I finally queried:

"Excuse me, do you happen to be a nun?"

"Yes I am," the pleasant Sister smiled.

After sharing conversation, I learned that *she* too was a Sister of Mercy. She was also an English teacher who knew Sister Margaret Mary. I was excited when I told her I remembered all the literary terms that we had learned.

"I especially remember the meaning of *oxymoron*."

The friendly nun replied, "Give me an example."

"A Sister of Mercy"

I've never heard a nun laugh so hard.

---

### How to spot a Nun:
- They always travel in threes.
- Most days, they dress like it's Easter Sunday.
- They have a warm, heavenly disposition which turns to a sneer when they see unruly children.

---

Good joke tellers are elite performers. They are able to paint pictures; they can relax and execute; they possess unique, trained skills and they can conquer the fears of the stage. Performing is more than executing a skill. Performing is executing that skill while others are watching.

# Golf

Many coaches and athletes play golf for the same reason I play the piano. It is a skill which requires tremendous mental concentration, technique and emotional maturity. By athletes and coaches mastering the discipline of golf, they become even better athletes and coaches. Years ago, I was an avid golfer.

*At least 90% of all putts that are short do not go in the hole.*

That's probably a conservative estimate. As a golfer, that proverbial image that I crafted was one of my favorite thoughts that helped me eliminate short putts.

Back when I was walking in the metal spiked shoes of a golfer [*it was that long ago*], I was introduced to a concept that really helped my game. **One thought**. My thought after addressing the ball, was "Finish". I had a visual picture in my mind that I associated with that single thought. The golfer was at ease, in a balanced posture with his hands held well above his head and his shoulders turned toward his target. I felt that I could predict how good of a shot a golfer had struck by the degree of perfection in his "Finish" posture. I tried to maintain that image in my mind throughout the execution of my stroke. That single thought was the final thought of my routine and told me that, "it was time to go.!"

In my view, every single football technique has its own specific **single thought**, prior to its execution. When the player experiences brilliant execution, the perceptive performer and coach will pause and make note of the effective single thought. The athlete then, will associate these positive thoughts during practice to develop habits that can be executed during the game.

When a performer's thoughts become multiple, and his emotional state becomes variable, the execution often suffers. A reporter once asked former Tampa Bay Buccaneers Coach John McKay about his team's lousy execution.

"I'm in favor of it," quipped McKay.

> "The oldest, shortest words – "yes" and "no" – are those which require the most thought."
> **Pythagoras**

# Piano Players and Pianists

Many people can play the piano. Few of them are pianists. Volume and texture control are critical characteristics of the piano; consequently, the keys are not played with the same techniques as a typewriter, harpsichord, organ or even an electric piano. A pianist can play the same notes as an amateur piano player; but, his sound is as different as day is from night.

Pianists are trained with various techniques; oftentimes, the techniques are related to their culture. Skilled listeners can distinguish a pianist who was trained in classical Russian, British, Austrian or American traditions. Boris Berman wrote in his book, <u>Notes from the Pianist's Bench</u>, about the relationship of culture and piano pedagogy. Berman compares traditional Russian techniques with traditional Western European techniques as they were taught in Germany, Austria and France. He compares the piano to a drawer. Berman maintains that Russians push on the keys, as if they are pushing the drawer inward; the others pull on the keys, as if pulling the drawer outward. These technique differences contribute to different tone colors; one is sharper, the other is more legato. Berman recommends that pianists master both types of skills in order to perform a universal repertoire.

Various cultural traditions take substantially different approaches to learning new music. A typical American learns the right hand and the left hand separately. After each hand is competent, the hands are put together. Other traditions, as often taught in Western European cultures, encourage playing slowly with both hands together immediately after the rhythms and fingerings are secure. Playing with both hands together encourages a more unified sound. After the piece is learned, it is still very useful to go back and polish each hand. My ears can usually identify the tradition in which a pianist was trained.

Music is an expression of culture; a culture's music is an extension of its language. Often, it's possible to guess the nationality of a composer by listening to his music. From his birth, the composer is influenced by his native language and the folk music of his homeland. Cultures with vowel rich languages (Latin, Italian, Spanish) are represented with legato (smooth), flowing music filled scales and arpeggios. Sharp, pointed music can be found in cultures whose language contains a lot of consonants (German, Russian). Blurred music, like impressionism, can be found in cultures with blurred language diphthongs (French). Even a composer's instrumental music is influenced by the nature of his culture's language.

The musician who acknowledges that music is more than notes on a staff, has an advantage. Every piece of music tells a story, shares an emotion or makes a statement. By understanding the art, science, history, technical mechanics and the sociology of music ... a musician gains insight into the interpretation of a mature performer.

Lee Galloway is a pianist, composer and educator who resides in the San Francisco Bay area. His recording, "Soothing the Soul," is a collection of popular classical pieces that are both relaxing and inspiring. He has great balance between his right and left hands. The great pianists create audible separation between the hands, almost as if two musicians are performing on separate instruments. In order to hear the melody, the right hand must be played louder and with different texture than the left hand. Unfortunately the thick, long strings on the left side of the piano produce more volume than the short, thin strings on the right side. Creating a full, lyrical melody with the right hand requires skillful technique since the pianist must work against the piano's inherent mechanical disadvantage.

During a recent visit to the Bay area, I contacted Lee to see if he was interested in offering a lesson to his audiophillic [*new word*] fan. We played for three fascinating hours, but at one point during the lesson he shared a great mental image:

"I imagine that the right hand is playing the piano in this room, while the left hand is playing a different piano in a closed room down the hall.  I try to create that sound."

BRAVO!

> "BRAVO!" ... the greatest compliment a listener can give a musician.  Watch his eyes light up when you say "Bravo!"

Lee's comment had great meaning for me as it was the perfect image.  Identifying and performing the "single thought" that elicits the correct response is the ultimate accomplishment for the coach and his performer.

# MASTER MOTIVATORS

Occasionally, the coach has to be the performer. Part of a coach's job is to inspire his players to raise their energy level for elite performance. Football coaches are especially skilled at motivation since football is an intense game that requires exceptional courage and grueling effort. The football player has to perform despite fear, injury and fatigue. Sometimes a great performance by a skilled coach is required.

Woody Hayes was the Hall of Fame Head Football Coach at Ohio State University from 1951-1978. Woody won five National Championships and thirteen Big Ten titles. He was a tuff, determined man who was able to inspire his team to assume his personality.

When practice wasn't going well, Woody would erupt. Sometimes he would get so mad he would take off his ball cap and literally rip it in half. Other times, he would remove his watch and stomp it to pieces on the ground. These stunts would inspire the players to increase their efforts. As it turned out, Woody kept an old watch in his locker which he wore when a rage was planned. He also kept a razor blade in his locker so he could cut the stitching in his hat before practice …. before his performance.

Such examples of Woody should not diminish how tuff he was. He would always wear a short-sleeve shirt on the football field, even if the temperatures were freezing. His coaches were not permitted to wear gloves even in the winter time; if he caught a coach putting his hands in his pockets, he would have the coach's pockets sewn shut. He never showed weakness to his team, and his team never played with any.

Bo Schembechler was every bit as intense as his mentor Woody Hayes; perhaps Bo stole a page from Woody's playbook. After working for Bo as a graduate assistant for just two seasons (1985-86), I could have filled all of these pages with great stories defining the master motivator.

In 1985, Michigan was holding a tight lead over Ohio State, but the tide was turning. Ohio State was taking control of the game and something needed to be done. Late in the fourth quarter, a controversial call was made by the referees. Bo went absolutely berserk. He threw his headset to the ground and stormed onto the field getting face-to-face with the face of the referee. I thought he had lost his control, his poise and perhaps our Team's chances of winning the game. After being pulled back to the sidelines, Bo put on his headset:

"Well let's see how the boys respond now," Bo said in a calm matter-of-fact tone followed by a chuckle.

His outburst was planned. It was a defining moment. From that point forward, the Michigan Team played tuff, aggressive football and pulled away from Ohio State 27-17.

Lots of coaches try to play the "tuff guy" role, but few are able to get their players to respond. The final conversation I had with Bo, prior to his passing, included the question:

"Bo, you used to coach the players so aggressively," I said, "but they loved you?"

Bo replied, "you can coach any way you want provided that the player knows you sincerely care about him."

*I knew that, I just needed to hear it one last time.*

# More Bo

In 1986, Michigan was preparing to play Coach Hayden Fry's team at the University of Iowa. Iowa had a tremendous home record; part of their success was attributed to Coach Fry's mental tricks. Fry was a Psychology major in college. Interestingly, the visiting team's locker room was painted pink. PINK! PINK?!! You can imagine what effect that had on the testosterone-filled football players who were preparing to compete against Fry's team that afternoon. Rather than invoking fear into their opponents, Iowa induced apathy.

Coach Bo had other ideas that he learned from the college of hard knocks. He sent some coaches to the locker room the night before the game and wallpapered the room with white butcher paper. Bo was not going to lead a pink, apathetic team onto the field. His team was going to play passionately and aggressively. *They always did.*

> "I never saw a man go to a fight with a smile on his face."
> **Bo Schembechler**

I came to Michigan in 1986, the year following Bo's worst season. The record was .500; Bo never had a losing season. After the season, some staffers would tell Bo that he needed to be more **positive**. One day during spring practice, The Team was sluggish: dropped passes, penalties, missed blocks and tackles. Bo called The Team together.

"My Coaches tell me that I need to be more positive," said Bo.

"Well I am positive! .... I'm positive that we stink. Now let's start the practice over again."

That year, Michigan finished ranked third in the nation. Bo had a way of being very sarcastic with words that you would think would crush the player's psyche. He had, in fact, just the opposite effect. When Bo said, "you're the worst player to ever play at Michigan," the player interpreted it as, "gee, Bo thinks I can be really good." *It was weird, but true.*

Under Bo, no individual was more important than The Team. At Michigan, "The Team" was always spelled with capital "T's". I think it was Bo's response to Woody Hayes, the arch rival, at The Ohio State University.

> "No player, no coach is greater than The Team."
> **Bo Schembechler**

# Breathe

Willie Anderson, my great offensive tackle, was an astute competitor.

"Most guys forget to breathe while they are blocking," Willie once told me.

I never really thought about the importance of breathing during the strain and exertion of blocking.

"When they stop breathing," thought Willie, "their feet and hands stop moving. They tighten up. They become tense."

Tension can cause a performer's body to lock up. By controlled and focused breathing, the performer can use flowing bodily movements. Singers, wind instrumentalists and stage actors all know how to breathe properly. I recall how Sister Marion Dimino, my high school chorus director, taught us how to breathe.

1. Inhale through your nose and mouth.

2. Keep your shoulders level; don't rise up.

3. Fill your lungs with your stomach and intercostals muscles.

4. Keep the tension in your gut as you release the air with control.

5. Exhale through your mouth.

Over the years, I've been amazed at the number of athletes who don't know how to breathe properly. Willie was right. Even pianists need to know how to breathe properly; it's an important skill for reducing and overcoming muscular tension.

"What will you give me if I empty the dishwasher?" my daughter asked.

"Air," I replied.

**Pavlo Sasha**

# Complete Thoughts

Have you ever been to a child's band concert at an elementary school? Perhaps you've experienced the whole band entering together on the first note of the piece at the conductor's direction. After the entrance, however, everything falls apart as the following notes fade away or get jumbled by the competing instruments. Chaos! Sometimes it sounds like someone singing with marbles in his mouth.

At the beginning of a musical line, the skilled musician thinks not about the first note, but rather visualizes the shape of the musical phrase. In other words, less skilled musicians will think about getting their first note right. This thought process makes the melody choppy and not very artistic. There's a difference between playing music and making music.

We have a cantor at our church who sings the first note of a phrase and then looks to the pianist, making sure that the entrance was right. Whenever the cantor sings and then glances at the pianist before continuing, I want to stand up and scream,

"When it's time to sing ..... just sing!"

Many musicians misunderstand the role of the accompanist. When a soloist performs, it is the responsibility of the pianist or orchestra conductor to adjust to the soloist's changes in tempi (speed)

and dynamics (volume) . I've found that many times the soloist thinks the accompanist is "in charge". This leads to a hesitant, sputtering performance. Although the soloist and the accompanist work out the specifics through rehearsal, ultimately the soloist should take the lead.

Some football players will get to their assignment and act tentatively until they are sure that other teammates have arrived. I want to scream, [*I'm already standing up*]

"Please...just play!"

The football player who thinks about taking a great first step will ultimately not get to his spot properly. In practice, it is important to break down and train each specific movement, but when it's time to play, then he should just play. The key is to flow through movements in an expressive, non-mechanical, fashion. When playing, the skilled performer visualizes the entire technique so that he will transition smoothly and flow through its execution.

"Play the music, not the instrument."
**Unknown**

# Herb

Herb Deromedi was the Head Football Coach for the Central Michigan Chippewas from 1978-1993. He was so successful that he is the winningest coach in the history of the Mid - American Conference and one of the winningest coaches in college football history. [*"Winningest" is actually not a real word; but, it should be.*] In 2007, he was inducted into the College Football Hall of Fame. It was an honor to work for Herb from 1987-1991.

In 1991, Central Michigan, a small Division I school, was slated to play the powerful Michigan State Spartans. State was the defending Big 10 Co-Champions and one of the nation's top ranked teams. Central Michigan's squad was mostly composed of players who weren't good enough to be recruited by Michigan State. The matchup was so lopsided that the Las Vegas odds makers did not even set a betting line for the game's final score.

The week leading up to the game, I was surprised to observe Herb's approach. Typically Herb is a passionate, competitive man. That week, however, he encouraged the team to just do their best … that the outcome didn't matter.

Jim Sandy, one of Herb's former players, gave the chapel sermon to our nervous team on the morning of the game. His theme was David and Goliath. We obviously weren't the giant. *Jim even passed out rocks!* I took one and put it in my pocket. I was ready to fight if called upon.

During team warm-ups, I was sick to my stomach. I tried not to look to the other end of the field as the teams stretched in formation. The Spartans looked liked a war machine and we looked like a band of brothers. Usually, I can't wait for the game to get started; *I couldn't wait for this one to get over.*

Herb gathered the team together in the locker room before the opening kickoff. The tension was thick and the moment was uncertain. This time Herb sang a new song to the anxious team kneeling before him:

"Just remember," Herb said, "Michigan State didn't recruit you guys because they didn't think you were good enough." "Now is the time to prove them wrong."

The locker room exploded. The Chippewas manhandled the Spartans 20-3. The victory was even more decisive than the scoreboard indicated. *Brilliant.*

I still have David's rock and have carried it in my shaving bag for 20 years. It's one of my favorite possessions in the world.

And, by the way, Herb plays the piano, too.

# Proactive Performance

Athletes can perform reactively or proactively. In basketball's man to man coverage, a defensive player covers his man wherever he goes. Well, not really. Not really at all. No defensive player in sports is able to cover a man by himself without bounds. Typically, a defender will cover half of the man to prevent him from going to the inside or the outside. Such a defender is acting proactively.

A reactive offensive lineman sets up and mirrors his opponent wherever he goes. A proactive offensive lineman sets on a path to a spot and forces the defender to adjust his path.

A reactive teacher who encourages wide open class discussion risks an unpredictable response from her class. A proactive teacher will define limits and boundaries for focused class discussion.

A reactive musician will wait to hear the other instruments play before joining them. But, the proactive musician will come in on time and perform while he trusts the other performers.

A reactive quarterback will wait for the receiver to break off his route before throwing the ball. A proactive quarterback knows his wide receivers body language so well that he will throw the ball even before the receiver breaks.

Ultimately, the performer identifies the component that allows him to perform proactively: the basketball player's position, the offensive lineman's spot, the teacher's boundaries, the musician's rhythm and the wide receiver's body language. Reactive performance is tentative and uninspiring; proactive performance is powerful and focused.

> "Fortune befriends the bold."
> **John Dryden**

# Ronald Reagan and Speechmaking

[*This book is not about politics.*]

I think it's fair to say that Ronald Reagan was the greatest orator of our time. He was eloquent; he was at ease; and, he could inspire. Before entering politics, Reagan was a Hollywood Actor. In his book, <u>An American Life</u>, Reagan shared some secrets about speechmaking. A well crafted movie had a great beginning and an even better ending; what happened in the middle was less significant. The same was true in speech making, or in writing a book. [*Wait until this one ends.*] Think back if you can recall any of Reagan's speeches. He almost always shared a warm, convincing story that was inspiring.

It's disappointing to watch a presenter give a great speech only to close it with a weak ending such as:

"Well, I will be around all afternoon, if anyone has any questions for me. Thank you."

Unfortunately, I've attended too many of those types of presentations.

The great speech maker has the ability to end his speech in an inspiring way that crescendos into applause. Many of us learned this obvious technique in a college public speaking course. But,

I rarely find great endings in real life speeches. My advice to speechmakers, whether it's in the business conference room, in the classroom or on the pulpit is to plan your ending before you start. Like a good playwright, be sure to subtly foreshadow your ending during the body of your speech.

The same advice is true for the musician. If the program starts and ends great, you have a great chance of pleasing the audience. Choose your music with this in mind. Encores should be inspiring, not *aren't you done yet?*

Perhaps my best advice to aspiring speechmakers:

Stop talking *before* the audience stops listening.

A short, inspiring talk that leaves the audience wanting more is more effective than a lengthy talk that covers everything. *Public speaking can be a rush.* I sense that a lot of speakers enjoy their moments of glory in front of the crowd. Some continue to bask in their glory until they sense that the audience is bored; once bored, those speakers quickly wrap up their speech. The best approach is to wrap up your speech while the audience is still interested.

I inject tricks into every one of my speeches that I call **tidbits**. A tidbit is a piece of trivia or an interesting point that might be unrelated to the topic. Tidbits can be funny, off the wall, passionate, or intellectually stimulating. A complete tidbit list spans all the emotions. When I feel the presentation drag, I go to my tidbit list. If the audience is bored, it's MY fault. It's my job to keep my classroom interesting. Once I have the audience's attention again, I can return to the topic at hand.

A speaker is an entertainer. A speech is like a good movie filled with twists, turns, suspense, tragedy and jubilation! By crafting the introduction, the ending and the tidbits, you are able to take the audience on an emotional roller coaster ride. Usually the most exciting rides are the best speeches.

> "Speeches that are measured by the hour will die by the hour."
> **Thomas Jefferson**

# Audiences

Focused performers are able to concentrate completely on the task at hand and ignore external variables. Recently, while giving a presentation to music students at the Ohio State University, I posed the question:

"Do any of you play differently when you see a professor who you respect walk into the room?"

Without prodding, several students nodded their heads in a way that you just knew they tensed up when that esteemed professor entered the room. Performers are notorious for wondering how the audience is judging them. When my children were young athletes, they would watch me in the stands during the game as much as the ball. Most performers grow beyond that stage; unfortunately, some continue to keep their eyes in the stands more than on the field.

During the summer, I coordinate several high school football camps. I'm startled when some of my coaches change their eye focus from the players they are coaching to me when I come by to observe their drills.

If you're a teacher, don't you find it odd when the student teacher is teaching to the principal who is in the room observing the class?

Athletes who listen to the booing and heckling of the crowd can lose confidence in their performance. Musicians and actors who enter the stage and evaluate the size of the audience are doomed for failure.

A few years ago, I was fortunate to have a home plate seat at a Cincinnati Reds game. I was, it seemed, 10 feet away from the batter's face. I could see his eyes, feel his sweat, and hear his breathing … his grunts and groans. I was amazed by the eye burning focus of a Major League Baseball batter at the plate. Once he sets his feet solidly in the box, he focuses his eyes; and, his head doesn't move.

Ultimately, great performers are able to focus on the task at hand. Great NFL performers are able to concentrate solely on their own personal matchup. When the mindset is right, that matchup could take place without a crowded stadium or fans on television. Thoughts of the audience must be eliminated and replaced with competitive thoughts about the performance itself.

"The only thing that's important," Albert would say, "is the music!"

> "I detest audiences. I think they
> are a force of evil."
> **Glenn Gould**

# In the Womb

I've played baseball and softball with guys who were great hitters in the batting cage, but lousy at the plate in game situations. The same is true with some stellar bullpen pitchers, great shower singers and practice room musicians. Something happens when some performers leave the confines of their tight practice surroundings and step onto the wide-open spaces of the stage. Sometimes the performer on stage feels like the emperor with no clothes on.

When I perform, I stake out my perimeter. If I'm playing the piano, I imagine that I am still confined to the small living room where I practice on my grand piano. I encourage football players to not get lost in the stadium, but to play within a small mental circle on the field. The same should be true for the baseball player who feels comfortable being confined to his imaginary batting cage or his bullpen.

From the womb, nothing from the outside can enter. The performer blocks entrance of negative thoughts into the womb. If a bomb explodes, a baby cries, a fan boos or someone in the audience has a coughing fit, then such distractions never reach the performer's mind. Inside the womb, the performer entertains the confident visions and the warm feelings of positive, elite performance.

# Centering

When I first began playing the piano publicly, my concern for the audience's reaction was an added stress on my performance. Being an NFL football coach made the situation more difficult. When you are a public person much is expected; sometimes the expectations are too great. Conquering stressors, however, is one of life's zesty challenges.

**Centering** is the ability to gain total mental control. Other words are mental focus, concentration and even some components of mental tuffness.

> "Tuffness is not only what you do to someone else, it's also how much you can take."
> **Howard Mudd**

A mentally tuff individual can perform while the fans are booing; the coach is riding his backside; or the game situation is unfavorable. Part of mental tuffness is the performer's ability to center his focus. I have a routine prior to a performance whether it's a piano performance, presenting a speech or coaching the big game. This routine combines thoughts I addressed earlier:

1. **In the womb**. Stake your fence around your comfortable perimeter. Don't let anyone or anything inside.

2. **Solid Base**. Establish a firm, relaxed posture that allows you to have complete control of your body.

3. **Breathe.** Exhale the stress away. Feel all the tension leave your muscles as you develop *relaxed tension.*

4. **Single thought.** Find that mental image that you associate with positive elite performance.


This routine can help the performer gain control of the performance, rather than, allowing his performance to be consumed by the environment. Whatever particular routine works for an individual performer, it needs to remain consistent and must be rehearsed.

> *I've confronted the enemy and the enemy is Me.*
> **Pavlo Sasha**

# Tennessee Fainting Goats

Tennessee Fainting Goats are a bread of meat goats that don't handle stress very well. When scared, their bodies seize and they exhibit temporary paralysis. They suffer from a genetic condition called **myotonia congenita**; it's believed to be caused by a chloride deficiency preventing the muscles from relaxing versus flight or fight stimuli. When frightened, they lock up and collapse. *I would like to be a wolf attacking this herd.*

Stress causes the hands to shake, the voice to tremble and the knees to wobble. How does the pitcher prepare his next pitch when he has just walked a batter to load up the bases? How does the singer hit high C while her legs feel as if they are going to collapse? How does a salesman continue to give his final plea while his client appears intimidating and disinterested? How do you continue to perform while the world is caving in around you?

Anxiety of performance can overwhelm a performer. Earlier we identified Vladimir Horowitz and Glenn Gould as two concert pianists who feared the stage. But, unfortunately, there's quite a list of celebrities who suffer from stage fright including: Shania Twain, Barbra Streisand, Donnie Osmond, Sir Laurence Olivier and Ozzie Osborne. Ricky Williams (Miami Dolphins) and Zack Greinke (Kansas City Royals) are athletes who have dealt with stress-related issues. The condition of a performer being overwhelmed by stress is sometimes identified as **Social Anxiety Disorder.**

Stress-induced responses during a performance are different than those experienced prior to a performance. Typically, a performer has both time and routine to establish his pre-performance centering techniques. Stress recovery during mid performance, however, is very difficult and requires mental discipline. The performer needs to associate a single thought to place him back in the womb immediately. The thought I use is *"breathe"*. As I focus on my breathing, I feel the stress leave my shaking extremities.

Unfortunately, mental thoughts and images cannot overcome the severe effects of myotonia congenita. The rare condition, experienced by the Tennessee Fainting Goats, is also found in dogs, cats and even humans. Some cases of stress induced performance anxiety have been controlled through therapy and medication. Most people, however, can center their focus and control stress induced panic attacks with practice, experience and confidence.

> "Courage is resistance to fear, mastery of fear, not absence of fear."
> **Mark Twain**

# I will make Mistakes

Some people, like myself, take themselves too seriously sometimes. The driven, achievement-oriented types sometimes have difficulty overcoming mistakes. They expect perfection from themselves and from others. Sometimes we are difficult to deal with.

There has never been a perfect human performance. Even a pitcher who threw a perfect game (no hits, no walks and no runs) threw some pitches that were slightly off the mark. Concert pianists perform such difficult music that it's impossible not to make at least a slight error. Unfortunately, if you keep the memory of the mistakes in your mind, you will inevitably experience more mistakes. Mistakes can have a viral effect. To play NFL football, or any professional level sport or art form, you need to have a short memory.

A year ago, I was fortunate to have a backstage pass for a professional piano performance. Six world class pianists entered the stage confidently, performed brilliantly, and then left the stage with their same confident aura. Once backstage, however, every one of them was mad. They were disappointed with their mistakes that only they could detect. I wanted to say:

"Hey, that was a great job!"

They were, however, deep in conversation with their third person. Their standard was high; their tolerance was low. I found this startling behavior to be enlightening.

Professional football players and their coaches are never satisfied. Every Sunday, the hope is to play the perfect game. That elusive game, unfortunately, never comes. Even a victorious game is littered with mistakes. Mondays, following an NFL game, are never enjoyable; the coaches and players review the game videos and relive the mistakes of the previous day. The goal of watching game video is not to persecute, but to improve for the next opportunity. Unfortunately, that next opportunity will include mistakes; but, the frequency of the mistakes should be reduced.

Every year, we host some recitals at our home to benefit the College Conservatory of Music. Our walls have been painted richly because of these soirees. This past fall, we hosted an adult student recital. As I stood before the audience of anxious performers and welcomed them to our home, I said:

"Ok, we're all going to make some mistakes tonight."

A look of relief flashed across the crowd's faces. Hopefully, my comment helped relieve some tension and eliminate some self-inflicted wounds.

I've found that most of my performance mistakes are the result of being distracted by random thoughts entering my mind.

"Think forward," Albert has told me repeatedly. "Concentrate only on the music."

I asked Albert an honest question recently. Albert had just performed a 60 minute solo recital at Steinway Hall in New York City.

"When you're on stage, how many times are you distracted by random thoughts entering your mind?"

"None," Albert confidently replied.

*Wow!*

To think that a concert pianist can hold his mental focus for 60 minutes is unimaginable. Not once did he have a human thought (It's too hot; I heard that gum wrapper, etc...). It's almost impossible. Albert was sincere.

As a result of my question, we began a new exercise. My goal was to perform an entire piece at home without allowing a single, external thought. I would remain centered the entire piece and concentrate solely on the music. The moment an external thought entered my head, I would stop and mark the music score at the spot. Then, I would start again from the beginning and try to better my last attempt. The first time I tried this exercise; there were 27 markings on my score. It took me 28 times to play an entire piece of music with a centered mindset!

Someday, I will try this exercise with my daughters sticking their fingers in my ears.

"A man may make mistakes, but he isn't a failure until he starts blaming someone else."
**John Wooden**

# "The Freak"

Willie played against "The Freak" (Jevon Kearse) at least a dozen times throughout their college and NFL careers. Jevon was a three time Pro Bowler and the 1999 AFC sack leader. "The Freak" was, as his nickname describes, a gifted physical specimen. Tall, lean, muscular, fast, and strong with long arms ….. Kearse was an intimidating character to look at.

Willie had unbelievable success in his personal matchup versus Kearse. I don't believe Kearse ever beat him. It was uncanny.

One day I asked Willie, "What's your secret to blocking "The Freak?"

"I never look at him," said Willie.

*I was dumbfounded.*

Willie knew that if he looked at "The Freak," then he would be intimidated by his physique; Willie would possibly make a technical error in an attempt to compensate for his "freak-ness". Willie knew that as long as he took the proper blocking angles, that geometry was on his side and he couldn't be beat. Willie rightfully believed that it was more important to concentrate on himself than what "The Freak" could do to him.

We train professional athletes to possess technique that is so clean that it will work against the superior opponents. The player must believe that his technique is more important than the prowess of his competitor. Often times, a player will lack self-confidence and will try to compensate by creating a new technique. Even if the athlete loses, he will minimize his losses by staying true to himself. To help prevent the athlete from over compensation, wise coaches don't hype a great opponent. They display trust in their player and they encourage the player's confidence in his skills.

> "Conquer yourself and you will conquer the opponent."
> **Japanese proverb**

# .....it's a small, small world ....

Have you ever been to Fantasyland at a Disney Park? If you've experienced the attraction: **it's a small world**, my guess is that it left an impression. Is that piece STILL playing in your head? Do you suffer from Disney's version of musical water torture? Did you try to jump out of the boat and swim to safety? Does that song ever end?!!

Hopefully you can relate the Disney attraction to a positive mindset about initiating a performance. To reduce some performance anxieties, try to:

> Imagine that the song/piece that you are about to perform is just another verse in the middle of an endless song.

> Imagine that the start of the game is actually the midpoint and you've already been playing for an hour.

I witnessed Albert experiencing a "small, small world" moment one evening prior to a performance. He was totally focused and humming the piece to himself the moments prior to his performance. He was already in the mood of the music before he entered the stage.

# "Kick their Butts"

"Yankees Beat Sox"

"Buckeyes Crush Gophers"

"Gators Spank Volunteers"

If you morphed from outer space and read these headlines, what would you think?

A concert review once reported that: "Beethoven slay the piano." [*as if the instrument was a dragon*].

Have you ever done so well that you "killed a performance, a game, or a presentation?"

Has a movie ever left you breathless?

Competitive performance is not for the meek. Successful performers attack with a dominant approach. Dominant performance is like breaking a horse. At first, the horse will not submit to the trainer. But through consistency, perseverance and plenty of imposed will by the trainer, the horse transcends from wild to docile.

Overly intense feedback, either positive or negative, can ruin the performer. Denny McKeown, a gardening expert, talks about "killing plants with kindness." Too much water or too much fertilizer can kill a plant just like withholding water and food.   The skilled coach is careful to push the performer to his limits to develop a stronger, and more competitive spirit.

Joe Paterno used to tell the team, "Football is a game of attrition.  Eventually one team says: Ouch! I've had enough."  That's the mental approach that a performer imposes on his opponent, his instrument or his audience.

*Someday the meek will inherit the Earth, but right now they're struggling.*
**Pavlo Sasha**

# Dreams and Positive Thoughts

A positive performer dreams with a positive mind set. Peter Ganshirt Psy.D. is a Sports Psychologist who works with the Bengals. Peter has performed significant research on peak emotional performance. In a team meeting one day, he shared his research with the team. Peter proposed a list of positive words for the players to consider for their emotional approach to competition:

| | | |
|---|---|---|
| Confident | Energetic | Calm |
| Anger | Alert | Determined |
| Fearless | Aggressive | Bold |
| Unhurried | Motivated | Fierce |
| Stimulated | Thrilled | Satisfied |
| Resolute | Pleased | Exhilarated |
| Focused | Dominant | |

He also posed a list of words that elicit negative competitive responses:

| | | |
|---|---|---|
| Afraid | Tense | Anxious |
| Dispirited | Dissatisfied | Panicky |
| Lazy | Tired | Indecisive |
| Uncertain | Apprehensive | Scared |
| Confused | Worried | Sluggish |
| Apathy | Irritated | Frustrated |
| Doubtful | Weary | |

Obviously, the exercise involved replacing negative thoughts with positive thoughts to create positive energy. The list of positive words is posted in my meeting room.

> "Become the change you want to see in the world."
> **Gandhi**

My high school coach was a great motivator. One time, he told our team:

"Think and dream positively. You will *become* what you dream about."

I was terrified by my coach's suggestion.

I was afraid that I would become a girl.......

# Timeless

*Note: Some will have little use for this section.*
*That's ok.*

**B**ach, Beethoven and Brahms, regarded as musical giants today, were certainly not always appreciated. In their time, they were progressive thinkers who wrote music that their contemporary audiences didn't embrace. A representative scathing review by John Ruskin, a British Music Critic, suggested:

"Beethoven sounds to me like the upsetting of a bag of nails, where here and there an also dropped hammer."

Although the nicknamed "3B's" (Bach, Beethoven and Brahms) were not fully appreciated in their lifetimes, their art was glorified to master status within 50 years of their deaths.

The **Bach Motif** is a four note theme that spells out his name **B..A.C.H**. (In German, his "B" is represented by a B flat and his "H" is represented a B natural). Bach was a clever, ingenious composer and he worked his signature motif into some important parts of his compositions. Over 400 compositions since Bach's death have included his signature motif as homage to the great master.

Unfortunately, the posthumous glorification of the 3B's didn't help them pay their bills.

Atonal music was created around the turn of the 20th Century, resulting from the compositional work of Arnold Schoenberg (1874-1951). It has continued to be a part of some modern concert music. Atonal music lacks a tonal center; although the pitches are highly organized, the tones appear random and the music sounds chaotic. *Sometimes atonal music sounds to me like a string of firecrackers popping inside a piano case.*

Concert music has been a mirror of society throughout history. The atonal forms paralleled the unsettled world of the 20th Century with the World Wars, the Cold War and the suppressions by megalomaniac political dictators. Atonal music's lack of lyricism, in my opinion, has led to its lack of mass appeal. The concert halls typically have fewer patrons for an atonal program of Schoenberg, Berg or Hindemith than a concert featuring the lyrical masters of Mozart, Mendelssohn or Chopin. Even after 100 years, the masses still don't like it.

Classical music fans are few in numbers, but are greatly devoted. In my opinion, atonal music has aided, to some degree, in concert music's diminished popularity. Many classical music fans fear about the future of our beloved art. *I fear not!* Modern classical music is thriving in the opera houses of Broadway and the electronic concert halls of Hollywood. Modern "classical" works like Phantom of the Opera, Wicked and Star Wars could have long term popularity. I believe that the timeless masters of our era will be the likes of: Andrew Lloyd Weber, Steven Schwartz and John Williams.

History is usually for the Monday morning quarterbacks, not the prognosticators. But, the future is always filled with clues from the past. 100 years from now, who will be the master composers? Since classical music is a mirror of society, modern art forms that represent contemporary ideals will prevail. Social ideals, such as the blending of cultures, are represented in the modern, expansive forms of music. Future musicologists will certainly study the 20th Century musical inventions of jazz, rock and roll and even rap music. [*Rap will be coming to Symphony Hall*].

If you accept that music is a mirror of society, then it's possible that atonal works will be the rage of the future. I fear that I'm like the foolish, forgotten critics who humiliated the brilliant works of Bach, Beethoven and Brahms, et al. Unfortunately I've tried, yet unsuccessfully, to open my ears enough to understand and appreciate atonal music. Like the masses, I don't care for atonal music. In the end, I'm just a football coach who likes lyrical music!

# Relentless

If you can visualize Tasmanian Devil, playing soccer, then you could visualize my daughter, Emily, when she was in third grade. My young daughters and I had a contest when they played soccer games. We counted how many times they touched the ball and they tried to break that record every week.

It's amazing how kids are different. Carolyn, the musician, played soccer more for the social aspects than for the competitive enjoyment. When Carolyn was young, she would touch the ball about ten times per game. If the ball happened to hit Carolyn where she was standing, then she would get a touch. Emily, on the other hand, was relentless. I think her record number of touches approached 140. She would blaze all over the field after that ball. During timeouts, she would run to the sideline and collapse on her back panting for the entire break. Once the timeout whistle was blown to resume play, she would spring up to her feet and sprint out onto the field eager for more action. From my perspective, as a father who is also a coach, it was a joyous sight to behold.

Carolyn, on the other hand, was in sixth grade when I made a "safe" bet with her. Wanting a laptop computer that cost about $200 dollars, she approached me with a deal. If she learned and memorized Beethoven's "Für Elise", would I buy her the laptop? I figured it was a very safe bet because:

1. The piece was beyond her ability level.
2. It probably would take her a full year to learn it.
3. Even if I lost the bet, it would be a great addition to her repertoire.

It took her two weeks to master the same piece that took me six months to learn. *I'm not betting her anymore.*

In my meeting room sits a big, beautiful leather reclining chair. Every week, I grade the players on their performance. One of the performance areas that I evaluate is the "finish" category. I assign points for various displays of extra effort. The player who gets the most "finish" points in the game gets to sit in the chair all week.

Perhaps you find it amusing that wealthy, professional athletes are inspired to play harder so that they can sit in the leather chair. Well, there's not much in life that a big man enjoys more than sitting in a big seat.    I recently gave a presentation to a group of high school coaches who coach the offensive line. Our lot, like our players, is typically a group of very large human beings. When we are guests in someone's home, they usually guard their wicker furniture with their lives. As the line coaches sat on their white, wooden folding chairs, I began my presentation:

"I want to inspire you so much today, that I keep you on the edge of your seats."

"But after looking at you guys and the size of those seats, I've decided to tone it down a little". *We chuckled.*

Relentless performers yearn for motivation and challenges. How do we as coaches, parents and managers inspire relentless aggressiveness in our performers? How do we as performers motivate ourselves similarly? More important than the prize, in the case of the leather recliner, performers typically love to compete. The rush of competition that Emily experienced as she chased the ball was exhilarating. If you're the type of parent or coach who is frustrated because your performers lack relentlessness, I suggest that you too make a game of it. Heck, even Mary Poppins knew that.

"Never throughout history has a man who lived a life of ease left a name worth remembering."
**Theodore Roosevelt**

# There's only 1 Bass in the Orchestra

Well, that's not exactly true, but my players don't know the difference. Usually there is more than one bass unless it's a small, Baroque-sized orchestra. A modern, full orchestra might have only six bass compared to over twenty violins.

The point is that one bass can be heard over the other instruments because the pitch frequencies are in ranges that don't compete with the other tones. Typically, the bass plays at least an octave below the other instruments, and can be heard clearly. Similarly, the single piccolo can be heard above the orchestra.

Effective communication requires that the listener can hear the speaker. I chuckle when I observe the young coach with laryngitis after one week of practice. I empathize with the student teacher who is frustrated on a field trip because the students aren't "listening." I sympathize with the football players who cannot hear the quarterback in a loud stadium.

Mothers have a way of screaming at their children so that the whole neighborhood will shudder, cower and hide. We hear pitches easily over background noises that are either high or low.

*As we age, we lose the ability to hear the high pitched tones. I like to give thanks to God for his compassionate plan for the married man.*

Listeners also discern tone textures. It's the only way I can explain why you can hear someone cough or open a gum wrapper during an orchestral concert, but not in a small crowded room filled with loud conversation. In that same small and crowded room, however, you would certainly hear someone burst out into song.

If you're a coach, a teacher, an actor, a speaker or an athlete who must communicate, then develop voice tones that can be heard. Adjust your pitch frequencies and textures. I require my offensive linemen to make their communication calls in deep tones and for their calls to be short syllables with lots of hard consonants. They really should be able to "grunt" their calls. The next time you watch a football game, listen to the quarterback bark out his cadence. If performed properly, his voice sounds very odd and unnatural, but, his voice carries easily over the roaring crowd.

"The empty vessel makes the loudest sound."
**William Shakespeare**

# No Distractions

The focused performer is able to eliminate distractions which interfere with his performance. The performer should enter the event with a single focus. The golfer might think only about his finish; he might have a rehearsed sequence of mental thoughts.

A curious coach who wonders how to counsel a performer about focused execution might try this fictitious exercise together:

"Tell me your single trigger thought that puts you in the zone," asks the Coach.

The performer pauses then replies, "Poise".

"Great," says the Coach. "Tell me the five most probable thoughts that could prevent you from completely focusing on your thought of *poise*."

After consideration, the performer offers:

"Where are my parents sitting?"

"I can't forget that my coach yelled at me during the timeout."

"The referees are killing us."

"I'm not sure our defense can stop the other team."

"Is my injured teammate going to be ok?"

The coach replies, "Do you feel it's possible to force yourself to eliminate thoughts about your parents, your coach, the referees, your defense and your teammate when it's time to do your job?"

"I think so," offers the performer.

"You must." insists the coach.

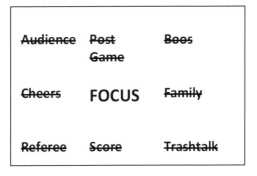

# Pull – Back

"Every time I play "Für Elise" for someone, I get nervous and start playing it faster and faster until I can't keep up." I told Albert.

"Always **pull-back** when you perform," Albert replied. "Perform a little slower than your maximum tempi you achieved in practice. This will help you remain in complete control. The audience won't know."

Great advice. It's advice for all human performers. It's counterintuitive to the theory that you *play like you practice.*

If a football player runs around like a chicken with his head cut off, he will make errors. You very rarely go *full* speed unless it is a last ditch effort. You go as fast as you can and still maintain control and balance. In fact, in most sports you usually have to keep some speed in reserve so that you can accelerate when necessary. It serves little purpose if a soccer player runs full speed at a ball but is unable to manage a coordinated kick.

> "A bird on a tether, no matter how long the rope, can always be pulled in."
> **Ronald Reagan**

# Richie

Rich Braham was an All American Offensive Tackle from West Virginia University in 1993. I went to his school for his tryout prior to the upcoming NFL draft. While at his school, I watched video tapes of his games and administered a lengthy interview which was basically an oral exam of his football knowledge. The final part of the day involved a workout for him to display his physical skills.

A normal pre-draft tryout for an offensive lineman consists of measuring his height, weight, flexibility, arm and hand lengths, followed by the vertical and broad jumps. On the field, the prospect is timed as he runs two 40 yard dashes, a shuttle drill and an agility drill. The final component is an assessment of his football skills as the player and the coach work together. I lined up against Richie as his opponent, holding a blocking bag.

"Don't be afraid that I'm the coach, Richie," I advised. "Block me as hard as you can."

Richie knocked me straight to the ground without even the slightest feeling of remorse or respect for the coach.

*I think I broke my neck*, I thought as he lay on top of me.

Slowly I winced up from the ground, while measuring all my body parts to be sure that they were still in working order.

*I need this guy on our team!* I smiled.

Richie ended up being drafted in the third round by the Arizona Cardinals in 1993. To my surprise, he was cut early in his rookie year and we moved immediately to sign him to our team. Richie had a great career. He was a tuff, physical performer with great competitive maturity. In 2006, after 13 great years, Richie retired in a ceremony at Paul Brown Stadium as one of the franchise's most respected players.

# Stereotypes

Is the athlete just a dumb jock?  Is the artist/musician just a softie?

**Joe Paterno** is not your typical football coach.  Joe is an Ivy League graduate with a degree in English.  Above Joe's desk hangs a portrait of Don Quixote and Sancho Panza, the famous windmill slayers.  *Joe himself slays stereotypes.*

Joe Paterno has won more football games than any other coach in the history of college football.  His accomplishments are staggering.  Joe has led a successful football program; additionally, he has also managed to produce:

> 15 Hall of Fame Scholar Athletes
> 41 Academic All Americans
> 18 NCAA Post Graduate Scholars

Joe Paterno is a teacher  and his subject matter is football.  Joe can converse on virtually any academic subject.  He follows politics.  Joe's ability to remember a person's name is uncanny; Joe only has to meet you one time.   He cares about the players as much as he cares about winning football games.  It's true.   I was there as a graduate assistant coach in 1983-1984 to see it.

Joe believes that sports and academics are related.  He wants the players to be successful at everything they do.   By succeeding in the classroom, the expectations of success are carried over to the football field. Probably, Joe's advice to aspiring performers is that they excel in all their endeavors.

> "Believe deep down in your heart that you are destined to do great things."
> **Joe Paterno**

Joe Paterno and **Mike Reid** have a lot in common. Joe coached Mike Reid at Penn State. Mike Reid was a great football player. In college, he was an All American, won the Outland and Lombardi trophies and was a finalist for the Heisman Trophy. Mike was a first round draft pick by the Cincinnati Bengals in 1970. Mike also owns a Grammy award and has composed seven hit singles. Mike is a pianist.

## OTHERS WHO MIGHT SUPRISE YOU:

**George Patton,** the heroic World War II General, was a ruthless commander. He was a tuff, controversial, driving man with little perceived compassion.

"A pint of sweat saves a gallon of blood."

Patton also wrote poetry. My guess is that Patton would have resisted the insinuation that he was *bridge brained* or *metro* ... maybe with a right hook.

**Winston Churchill** was the dynamic Prime Minister of England. His lengthy list of accomplishments included leading the Allied Forces to victory in World War II.

"It is not enough that we do our best; sometimes we have to do what's required."

Churchill was also a gifted amateur painter and won a Nobel Prize for Literature.

**Marv Levy**, the legendary coach of the Buffalo Bills, led his team to four Super Bowls and is enshrined in the Pro Football Hall of Fame. Most of his championship teams came towards the end of his career.

"The age factor means nothing to me. I'm old enough to know my limitations and young enough to exceed them."

Levy received a Master's Degree in English from Harvard University as well. He was probably the most famous coach to recite lines from Kipling, Emerson and Hemmingway at his team meetings and press conferences.

**Woody Hayes**, the Hall of Fame coach for Ohio State University was also a history buff. Woody hosted a television show that discussed military history and national security. Hayes also lectured on the subject at Universities across the land, including Harvard University.

"Without winners, there wouldn't even be any civilization."

**Garth Brooks** and **Toby Keith** are country music stars who also have athletic talents. Garth played minor league baseball and Toby was a college football player.

Perhaps, the subtitle of this book could have been titled **Stereotypes**. Hopefully, some readers with hidden talents have found comfort.

- If you are an artistic athlete who paints in the closet, then I encourage you to come out and paint where the light is brighter.

- Perhaps you're the coach or the teacher who is searching for a philosophy; I recommend that the best answers can be found in a mirror.

- Maybe you're a single-minded musician or stage performer; by broadening your vision, you will find inspiration in the unlikeliest places.

This is a book that has been part of my soul that I've needed to share. Thanks for coming with me. But, it's now time to "hang on". This ride is racing to the finish line.

# Willie and Stacy

Willie was entering his 13th season in 2008 with the Bengals. Throughout his career, he had established himself as the best right tackle in the NFL as he was named to four NFL Pro Bowls. Willie was not only a dominant player; he was the heart and soul of the Bengals franchise. He was the team captain for the majority of his career. Willie was responsible for many young players maturing to accept the responsibilities of an NFL athlete.

Willie was a charitable and religious man, often giving his time and treasure to his foundation that helped support disadvantaged children. On Thanksgiving, you would find Willie handing out turkeys. At Christmas time, he would share the joy with children as he showered them with gifts. During the summer, he would work with high school linemen teaching them football skills. Willie was, in a number of ways, one of the few special men to walk the face of the earth.

The evening following the 2004 NFL Draft, my wife and I were sitting on a neighbor's porch rocking in their chairs and enjoying the beautiful spring evening.

"Well Paul, did you draft any offensive linemen today," my wife Kathy asked.

"We drafted a guy named Stacy Andrews in the fourth round," I replied. "He has never started a football game in his life."

Kathy looked confused.

Stacy was an All American Hammer thrower from Ole Miss who would have a shot at being an Olympic athlete if he chose. Instead, he decided to play football during his junior and senior years for the first time in his life. In total, he played about 75 college football plays. Stacy was a natural right tackle, the same position that Willie played.

Willie befriended Stacy and effectively took him under his wing to help teach Stacy the NFL game. The NFL can either be a cut throat business or the greatest act of teamwork, depending on the chemistry of the team. Our offensive line has always operated in a manner that we share all information in our quest for greatness. Willie was Stacy's teacher.

After Willie's 12th season, it became apparent to me that young Stacy Andrews had overtaken the great Willie Anderson at right tackle. A combination of Stacy's youth and Willie's age, wear and tear were the reasons for this observation. At this time, I had to make the hardest call of my coaching career.

"Willie, we are going to go with Stacy as our starting right tackle," I said with a pit in my stomach and water in my eyes.

I evaluated, drafted and developed Willie. He became everything I believed about technical and focused performance. Willie helped make my career. We had discovered so much together and I learned as much from him as he did from me. He was the rock of our franchise. He was the best damn right tackle I had ever seen.

Willie was a great man, charitable and selfless. Out of his good spirit, he gave himself to Stacy and helped mold the man that would eventually replace him.

At that time, I initially wanted someone else in the organization to tell him. I could do practically anything with the exception of telling the greatest player I had come to know, that he no longer would be good enough. But it had to come from me.

"I understand," said Willie.

Once again, he was stronger than me.

# PIANOPALOOZA

**GAME DAY**. That's how I approached
**Pianopalooza.** Losing would not be an option
today. I was going to overcome the nerves that
ruined my first two performance experiences. In
fact, I had no choice. There was a feature article in
the **Cincinnati Enquirer**, *"Bengals Coach has a new
Forte: Piano."* The television stations were covering
the grand event. I might just have easily stuck a
*Kick Me* sign to my back. How was I sure that I
would overcome the jitters and not embarrass
myself publicly? I wasn't sure, not sure at all.

The hay, however, was in the barn; most of the work was done.

> The song selection of the rich Tchaikovsky piece, which would mask any mistakes, was comforting. So was the Brahms Waltz, the Lullaby Song that everyone would recognize and pleasantly hum along with us.
>
> The lessons and practices were intense and thorough. We knew the music completely. It wasn't going to be a mechanical issue that would unravel us; it would be a performance issue. With no audience, the music was beautiful. But then again, a lot of people can sing beautifully in the shower. It's another thing, altogether, to get up on stage and perform.
>
> The dress rehearsals went well. We made mistakes; but, we pushed through the mistakes.

Performance, however, is not about stacking hay. Many people can execute skills. Only skilled performers can execute under pressure. At this point, it was mental.

I only knew a routine that had worked for me in the past as a football player. When I was a player, and now as a coach, I have a routine that helps put me into a mindset for focused performance.

Protein only. I couldn't withstand the insulin surges that I get from the ups and downs of carbs. I ate my last meal four hours before the recital. Football coaches typically believe it's better to fight on an empty stomach; the blood and energy needs to be focused on the brain and the muscles, and not the belly. I also gently paced myself throughout the day with the caffeine from Diet Coke to keep my energy level constant.

Early in the morning, I practiced the music at super slow-motion tempo. The same way Rachmaninoff rehearsed Chopin's "Etude in Thirds". The same way NFL players will do a "walk through" practice the morning of an evening game.

I always wake up five hours before a football game. If we play at 1:00 pm, I wake up at 8:00 am. If we play at 9:00 at night, I take an afternoon nap and wake up at 4:00 in the afternoon to begin my morning ritual of a shower, meal etc. I followed my normal competitive routine.

Three hours before kickoff, I was alone by myself. Well actually, just Peter I. and I were alone. …..Tchaikovsky. [Pyotr Ilyich Tchaikovsky] As a college player, I listened to his "1812 Overture" before every game. No music was ever written as keener motivation for someone to play football than this great overture. It even inspired the "Bad News Bears". It was a flashback moment, but helped me to get in the right mood.

An hour and a half before kickoff, Albert and I rehearsed on stage. It was an intense practice, full speed and to a lather. We tried various tempi and were not afraid to try new expressions. We were not going to tense up tonight if something was different.

Before leaving, we positioned the location and height of the piano benches precisely where we wanted them since we were performing first. The physical foundation of all great performance begins with a solid, comfortable base. The stage crew was encouraged, well perhaps threatened is a better word, to not let anyone touch it.

*I am playing for Albert tonight. He is such a great teacher and has given me so much.*

*I will not let him down.*

*He will be disappointed if ......* immediately I think about the three most difficult spots in the program....the rapid fortissimo chords in the Tchaikovsky, the polyrhythmic section and the arpeggio finale of the Brahms.

*Oh no!* I thought.

*What if I mess those spots up?!!*

The piano is the ultimate challenge of mental focus. The only times I had trouble with those three spots was when my mind would drift for just a moment.

To think about something played, or going to be played, or what the audience thought, or ........ *But not tonight.*

We will take it one phrase at a time always focusing one measure ahead so that the phrases flow freely. No matter what, I will not be affected by anything that happens nor will I think too far in advance. I will play the white spaces on the page as beautifully as the black marks. I will finish the play until the whistle.

Thirty minutes and counting. I eat my Gatorade protein bar, as I do every Sunday 30 minutes prior to kickoff. Albert and I go to a studio and play the routine over and over again. Although we've made a few mistakes today, we've kept playing.

Ten minutes. Backstage. Crowd stirring probably, but I was completely detached. There was no crowd tonight. I would not look at the crowd, just as Willie would not look at "the Freak". The only concern in the world was the 10 foot area surrounding the piano that needed to be slain. Steinway was waiting for me. Pacing back and forth. 10 minutes seemed like 60. Humming the songs over and over again, keeping the music in my head. *I refuse to let any negative thoughts enter my mind.*

"What is the last chord?!! Oh my God! Albert, What's the last chord?" I implored.

"It's the same chord you've played thousands of times and never missed," said Albert. "Don't even think about it; it will play itself." Albert suddenly looked concerned, but tried to fake it.

"Thanks."

Five minutes. The Master of Ceremony approaches me and wants to talk about football. I ignore him and hum louder. He understands.

Two minutes, still backstage. I can hear the MC now. The program has begun. In the echoes, I hear "Football Coach". I cover my ears. *I'm not the Coach. Tonight, I'm the performer.*

**It's time.** Enter, bow, don't look at the audience ["*the Freak*"].

Me against the piano. *Cry Steinway.*

*The more you cry, the more beautiful the sound.*

*To the death.*

*Death by power, death by tenderness.*

*Nonetheless, Steinway…. Death.*

Seated. Hands set. *Have fun. Relax. Play Aggressively. Conquer.*

Beautiful sound. Perfect rhythm. Keep going. Think ahead. Tricky spot number one coming up and the hands start to shake. But, it's impossible to play rapid fortissimo chords while the hands are shaking.

*Breathe….*

*….Breathe….*

Hands relax. First spot down.


Tchaikovsky defeated. Now for Brahms.

The polyrhythm of the second tricky spot progresses without any consideration.

Nice crescendos. Different expression than we rehearsed; but, we're relaxed and it's beautiful.

*Oops!* C natural instead of C#.

*Oh no!*

My hands lock up, and I can feel a death grip racing up my arms to my shoulders. But, this is the exact moment why we rehearsed the piece hundreds of times. We slowly resolve the note back to its home key trying to make it appear as a planned modulation. Tension fades into resolution. Beethoven smiles. Brahms concurs.

My third person character took over at this point and the final arpeggios were as smooth as silk.

Final chord. Pianissimo.

*Euphoria.*

I shared my euphoria with everyone who wanted a piece of it. If it was a football game, we won 42-3 tonight.

After the show, I asked some friends and my family if they heard any wrong notes.

"No, not any," they said. "It was perfect."

My friend Michal knows music.

"Paul," Michal said, "the Brahms was the most beautiful piece of the whole evening."

"Did you know that piece?" I asked.

"Yes, I did," said Michal. "I've heard it many times before."

*Of course it was your favorite. It would have been my favorite, too.*

"Thank you," I nodded.

The adrenaline rush from the performance was like a football victory. While celebrating the victory at the ice cream shop after the concert, my daughter Carolyn, whose talent started this whole journey, noticed:

"Dad, was there one note that was wrong about halfway through the last song?"

"Ugh," I groaned.

Then I smiled.

*"We decided to let Steinway kick a field goal."*

To watch Pianopalooza go to:
**www.perform-coach.com**

Also at **www.perfrom-coach.com**

Future performance material (tidbits)  blogged

Bulk discount book orders for team, staff, company

Purchase Albert Mühlböck CDs

PERFORM

## GRAZIE

**PERFORM** is a self published book. A number of friends and professionals looked at the book for input at various stages along the way. It's said that, 'it takes a village to raise a child.' It takes a team of critics to write a book.... and a writer with thick skin.

**Rick, Tom and Jim Alexander**, my brothers. A band of brothers. Tight.

**Shirley Alexander**, my mother. My inspiration. The Education Champion.

**Willie Anderson,** a great player; a better man.

**Erik Bitterbaum Ph.D.**, SUNY Cortland President. Cortland's precious gem.

**Amy Boninio**, editor in chief. Writing coach extraordinaire. The *prima donna*. Still hates the way I spell tuff. Wishes that I organized everything in alphabetical order. Phrases drive her crazy. Two independent clauses must be separated by a semicolon; and, if a coordinating conjunction is used, it must be punctuated with a comma. Obviously, a Catholic school English teacher. ☺

**Michal Bonino**, Amy's brilliant husband. The

most generous couple on earth. Everyone should strive to be a Bonino.

**Jack Brennan**, Bengals Public Relations Director. Some helpful editing.

**Mike Brown**, his sincerity and support after reading the manuscript were inspirational.

**Daniel Coyle**, NY Times bestselling author... Lance Armstrong's War, The Talent Code etc. I sent Dan an early draft of my book; he really liked it and offered some good leads.

**Janelle Gelfand Ph.D.**, musicologist and dedicated classical music writer for the Cincinnati Enquirer. Her initial edit helped set the course of this project. Pretty fair piano player, too. *Brava.*

**Robert Greenburg Ph.D.**, composer, musicologist and lecturer. The Teaching Company. Everyone should teach like Bob. *Bravo.*

**Richard Hawley Ph.D.**, former educator and author of The Headmaster's Papers, Reaching Boys, Teaching Boys and 20 other inspiring books specializing in education.

**Robert Joseph**, a talented student at the Art Academy of Cincinnati. Robert designed and produced the covers, the illustrations and much of the photographic art. Keep your eyes on him... he will need a job soon. (He's good!)

**Charles LeTourneau,** classical music agent IMGartists. Contact Charles at Carnegie Hall Tower for my availability at symphony shows and performance-themed seminars.

**Marvin Lewis,** his broad smile after reading the book told me everything. A great inspiration, his big picture includes humanity.

**Albert Mühlböck,** Seek out his music at CDbaby or **www.albert-muhlbock.com**. (also link from **www.perform-coach.com**). A world class performer as a pianist and a teacher. Worthy of my greatest admiration.

**Ed Nietopski,** my high school coach. He hasn't read the book (yet) but his spirit is all over these pages. What a coach! (P.S. Hey Coach, my Catholic jokes were .... jokes)

**Michael O'Gorman**, "the Rowing Coach" is a youth football coach and a human database of sports psychology. One of my few coaching confidants in this project.

**Gary O'Hagan**, IMG Coaches agent. Inspirational.

**Don O'Hagan**, Gary's brother, and former

editor at Prentice Hall, who offered great publishing advice.

**Photography** of Coach Alexander at practice and Willie Anderson  printed with permission from the Cincinnati Bengals.

**Red,**  she didn't get to read it until after I published it.  I hope she likes it.  She likes surprises. (Also thx: MB, Mayhay and Emme)

**Rogers Athletic Company** and John Green

**Pavlo Sasha,** Pavlo (Latin: small: Paul); Sasha (Greek: leader:  Alexander).  No prologue or foreword. The game is over.  GO in peace.

**Steinway and Sons,** Irene Wlodarski and Anthony Gilroy (NYC) and Greg Kottmann (Premier Pianos, West Chester,  Ohio)

**Bob Surace,** reads a ton of this genre and his excitement excited me.  A very dear friend.  He said he would buy 10 books; maybe after seeing his name in print he will buy 20.

**Dennis Webster**, author of <u>Joey Bag of Donuts</u>, <u>Absolutely Wild</u> etc. and a great publishing resource.

*Mille grazie.*

# *the Cast of Characters*

Mary Beth  Carolyn      Emily   Kathy      Paul

Willie                    Albert

# About the Author

**PAUL ALEXANDER**, a veteran of 20 NFL coaching seasons, is currently the Assistant Head Coach and Offensive Line Coach for the Cincinnati Bengals. As a Bengals coach, he has developed four time Pro Bowl Tackle Willie Anderson and Pro Bowl alternates: Levi Jones, Eric Steinbach, Bobbie Williams and Andrew Whitworth.

Prior to the NFL, Alexander coached 10 years at the college level apprenticing under three Hall of Fame coaches including: Joe Paterno (Penn State); Bo Schembechler (Michigan) and Herb Deromedi (Central Michigan). Alexander was a Physical Education Major in college with a Minor in Music. While at SUNY Cortland, he was an Academic All American football player. He holds a Masters degree in Exercise Physiology from Penn State.

Coach Alexander has a passion for studying and developing human performance. He enjoys art, classical music, traveling and "camping" with his family whenever his crazy coaching schedule permits. His joy for his family's pack of dogs is questionable. He is also an adult piano student at the University of Cincinnati's College Conservatory of Music.

To contact the author's publicist:
coachpaulalexander@gmail.com

www.perform-coach.com

Made in the USA
Middletown, DE
16 January 2017